THE CUTTING HORSE

ISBN 0-9627181-7-3

Library of Congress Catalog Card Number 90-62650

Published by the National Cutting Horse Association
4707 Highway 377 South
Fort Worth, Texas 76116-8805
Phone (817) 244-6188

Produced by The Weller Institute For The Cure Of
Design, Inc.
P.O. Box 726, Park City, Utah 84060

Coordinated at NCHA by Patrick W. Steenberge.
Copy edited by John Wiebusch. Design by Don
Weller, assisted by Chikako Weller, using the
typeface Goudy Old Style. Printed and bound by
Sung in Printing Co., Ltd., Korea, coordinated by
Bolton Associates, San Francisco.

Randy Witte's essay first appeared in *The Western
Horseman Magazine*. The story, *Hub: Champion
Cutting Horse* by Robert H. Williams, can be ordered
from Eakin Press, P.O. Box 90159, Austin, TX
78709, $10 postage paid. The cutters' excuses are
used with the courtesy of the Oxbow Ranch.

Special friends of this project include Marvin
Thomas for initial information and encouragement,
Met and Lana Johnson, Lew Stevens, Kathy Thomas,
Robert Condie, Dennie Dunn, Zack T. Wood, the
NCHA Executive Committee, and Doc Baritz.

THE
CUTTING
HORSE

PHOTOGRAPHED BY
DON WELLER

FOREWORD BY
THOMAS McGUANE

TEXT BY
PATRICK W. STEENBERGE,
DON WELLER,
ROBERT H. WILLIAMS,
AND RANDY WITTE

SONG LYRICS BY
IAN TYSON

PUBLISHED BY
THE NATIONAL
CUTTING HORSE
ASSOCIATION

FOREWORD

Cutting has come a long way since 1898, when Sam Graves ponied old Hub behind a buggy for two days to the Cowboy Reunion at Haskell, Texas, where he won the first formal cutting horse contest. Still, some of the ideas of horsemanship exemplified by Hub and Sam Graves, ideas that were born on the 50,000,000-acre unfenced pasture called West Texas, still are very much alive today.

Cutting has expanded into a national sport, or national art form, depending on your point of view. But its origins always will lie indelibly in the range cattle industry. The standards of horsemanship and cattle husbandry derive from those of the western cowman who handled his stock as carefully as he handled himself. There is no more eloquent phrase in the NCHA rule book than "quietness in the herd," because the quietness referred to is one of strength and knowledge and creative restraint.

Some cutting horses have seen palm trees and some have seen glaciers. And there is scarcely a profession or occupation that is not represented among riders of cutting horses.

Yet the uniqueness of cutting remains undiluted. Like all great sports, you never get to the bottom of this one. Every horse is different, every rider is different, every cow is different. Seemingly invincible trainers go into sudden decline. Great horses quit or run off. Unknowns become famous in 2 1/2 minutes. Cutting is not show business or entertainment and its audience must make a serious attempt to understand it to enjoy it. Cutting is an extraordinarily strenuous attempt by man to understand the horse in the context of work.

Dwight Eisenhower once told his hosts on a Georgia plantation that he couldn't wait to get back to World War II to escape the pressures of quail hunting. And many a cutter has gone to work on Monday morning with the same sense of relief. At a cutting, nobody really cares about anything except how well you can show a cutting horse. In the long run, even in the most crowded coliseum, horse and rider are alone. Often the worst anxieties disappear with the first steps toward the herd. The frightened colt remembers his work when the cow is in front of him. Yet cutting is like the tar baby; few who touch it ever get loose.

On any given weekend, somewhere in Canada or Australia or the United States, the day is beginning and cutters are saddling or warming up their horses. In the early light, the bawling of cattle, the creak of trailer doors, and the murmur of conversations build to the ceremony of another cutting, another reenactment of the art and sport and history we all love.

Tom McGuane

MOVE
'EM
OUT

In the Beginning,
There Were Cowboys
and Cutting Horses

By Patrick Steenberge

The cutting horse was born of necessity long ago on the plains of the Old West. Since then, this living legend has earned distinction and respect on the range as the aristocrat of working cowhorses. From the early days of trail drives to modern-day cattle operations, the cutting horse has remained a ranching tradition—a living, working legend of the West.

The grand days of the big ranches in the United States had all but passed by 1890. Since the end of the Civil War, the open grass plains of West Texas had borne a breed of men and horses who worked the open range together. This was the era of the big cattle drives. Between 1877 and 1885, more than 1,000,000 head of cattle trampled the cattle trail through West Texas on their way to Dodge City, Kansas.

The heroes of that day are chronicled in western legend, while their brands are a part of America that embodies the spirit of the West. Burnett and the 6666 Ranch, Waggoner Ranch, the CO8, the Pitchfork, the Matador, Swensen Ranch. Grass was tall and plentiful. Barbed wire was non-existent.

Cattle were king, and the cutting horse was the knight of the kingdom.

A functional animal, the cutting horse enabled big country ranching to exist. He was as valuable to ranching then as the computer is to modern society.

His was a simple task by definition. With the guidance of his rider, the cutting horse would enter a herd of cattle quietly and deliberately. The rider methodically selected the individual cow to be cut, or separated, from the rest of the herd. And only the top hands earned the right to ride the best horses of the remuda, the cutting horses.

Without the aid of ropes, whips, or mechanical devices, the cutting horse drives one cow out from the herd. At the point at which a calf realizes she is apart from the others, her adrenaline begins to pump. Herd instincts take over and the animal attempts to dart back to the safety of the masses.

Standing in her way, performing his appointed task, is the cutting horse. His breeding and training have taught him that where the cow goes, so does he. And the game is on.

The horse controls the calf by a series of moves and counter moves, always a step ahead of the somewhat slower cow. The speed, agility, balance, and quickness of the cutting horse eventually wins out and the cow gives up. She then is kept apart by the other cowboys, whose job it is to hold the cut. The job done on that cow, the horse re-enters the herd and goes about his craft again, and again, and again, until the day's work has been completed.

The unique skills of the cutting horse long have been a source of pride on the range. It was this pride, sparked by the competitive spirit of the frontier cowboy, that led to the initiation of cutting competition in the 19th Century. Some of the first contests were held when boasting among ranch hands led to impromptu challenges.

With the staging of the first cutting horse contest for money, reputation no longer was the only thing at stake. This historic event was held at the 1898 Cowboy Reunion in Haskell, Texas. Twelve cutting horses were going after a purse of $150.

8

Les Bowman on Sonny Boy.

LEGENDS OF CUTTING
Ian Tyson

The legends were young
When the range was still open
And cattle still roamed on the land
And they watched and they listened
And they learned from the old ones
The business of making a hand.

And they still remember,
The days with the wagon
Working cattle in the old cowboy way
And though times have changed
The legends ride on
And they're still riding with us today.

CHORUS
Buster and Shorty
Matlock and Don,
Mr. Pat, he's still horseback
And still keeping on.
There's a new generation
And they're comin' on strong
But where would they all be today
If the legends of cuttin'
Had not shown them the way.

COWHORSE
MEMORIES

Scenes of the
Cutting Life...
in Words
and Pictures

By Don Weller

I started out several years ago to shoot a few photographs of cowhorses. That start became an odyssey that led to new friends, new places, new questions, new tests. The shooting is done, and the friends, places, questions, and tests remain, but now I am horseback, in the cows. The photographs in this book show jumps and sweeps, sweat and atmosphere. The words that follow were products of my journey, too. With the photographs, they hopefully will speak to you about what it's like out there in the world of four-legged creatures and the men and women who are just along for the rides.

EASTERN WASHINGTON STATE

In high school and college I roped calves in small rodeos on a horse named Sandy. He would tremble when his haunches felt the back of the box. He'd jerk his head left and right, refusing to look at the calf till he was ready.

When he would finally point his ears and freeze, giving his complete attention, I knew he was set. Then slam, bam, crash ... and we were flying across the arena, rope singing.

The roping was like throwing a rock into a 40-mile-an-hour head wind. A sudden stop, taut rope, two wraps and a half hitch. It all took, say, about 15 seconds. There was not a lot of sophisticated horsemanship in those seconds, either. Sandy had a tie-down to hold his head, a spur (left side only) for an accelerator, a jerk line for reverse, a neck rope for guidance. I never thought to ask him if he really enjoyed those four-hour midnight trailer rides for a few seconds of fast work. He didn't have much choice.

It was in this frame of mind that I saw my first cutting horse contest at a fair/rodeo in Colfax, Washington, in 1957.

A common ancestry links rodeo and cow cutting. Both involve a soft arena, horses, cows, and men. Both have turned old-time cowboy duties into sport. But there the similarities end.

In contrast to his rodeo counterpart, the cutting horse sneaks into a herd of cattle, separates one, and dances back and forth to prevent its return. Start stop, jump run, stop turn. Ears and eyes on the cow, head down, feet out, nostrils flaring.

The horse is on his own, smiling all the way, and the cowboy seems to be only a passenger. There is a legend about a cutting horse who continues to work a cow even though his rider has fallen off.

The horse's reactions are so quick that the information on cow movements that reaches his soft horse eyes barely has time to get to his little horse brain before he signals his giant horse muscles to react. Certainly those messages come too fast to have been translated by a rider via bit or spur.

I remember being impressed, and deciding that this must be cowboy horsemanship taken to the ultimate. But my focus remained on the slam bam of rodeo's roping events.

Out of college three years later, I sold my horses, tack, and trailer, left the Northwest, and buried all my memories under 25 years of adventures in the advertising wars in Los Angeles.

RURAL UTAH, THREE DECADES LATER

In early May, 1985 I drive to meet Marvin Thomas in Oakley.

Small farms line State Road 189 in northern Utah between the Wasatch Mountains and the High Uintas. It is fertile land. Grass grows. The cattle and the horses graze.

I park in the gravel and start toward the blue house. Everything is neat and looks new. The driveway that leads to the metal barn out back is made of crushed rock, not yet packed in, too new to be rutted, crunchy to drive on. Staked young 10-foot trees line the drive, about 20 feet apart. The corrals are made of pipe.

Two small dogs welcome me. They carry Australian sheep dog blood. They seem smart and are friendly.

Marvin is up the road, helping a neighbor. It's about 7 p.m. and the sun is low. The fields are turning green; in the late light the grass has a fluorescent quality. Snow-capped peaks are turning purple. The ground is pungent; nature is generous with her smells.

Three quarters of a mile away, a blue pickup is parked near a smoking ditch. Three men with shovels spread the fire farther and farther, burning the dead grass that chokes the ditch, and stamping out the fire that wanders too far. The first man points out Marvin.

Marvin is working late. There are lots of extra chores now that the snow has melted. He's been up early. He trains cutting horses for a living, and most days he's horseback by 8 a.m.

Marvin has these horses in his blood. My interest is genuine, and it is easy to encourage him to expound, he with the easy knowledge, deep blue eyes, and a western drawl.

Yes, cow cutting does most certainly still exist. I hear about the big money days of not many years ago when these horses fit the definition of a tax shelter. Cutters still are competing for more than 17 million dollars prize money annually. It can be an expensive sport. A horse good enough to compete in local cuttings will cost at least $4,000. And a world champion costs a small fortune.

Marvin says there are more than 13,000 members in the National Cutting Horse Association. The largest activity is in Texas, but all over the West and South there are contests every weekend--spring, summer, and fall.

He confides that they had a cutting demonstration at the Salt Palace rodeo (four horses) and afterward fans filled out questionnaires ranking cow cutting second behind bull riding as best liked events.

We talk about blood lines. The sires that were famous when I first discovered cutting horses 30 years ago, with names such as Leo, King, Three Bars, and Poco Bueno, now are great grandfathers of the current horses. They are bred for quickness, athletic ability, intelligence, and most of all, "cow sense."

We talk as the sun sets. The smell of the burning grass combines with the other smells of spring, taking me back to my rural youth; the conversation pulls my long-dormant love of western horses to the surface.

It's getting dark as we finish the ditch and climb into the pickup for a ride to the house. It's been five hours since Marvin got off his last horse, but I notice he still is wearing his spurs.

As I drive back to Park City, the sun is down and the landscape is black. But there is enough reflected light on the horizon, so that I can make out the snow-capped ski mountains ahead of me. No lights, no towns ... alone with Ricky Skaggs's music, whipping through the vast night. A quarter century of advertising meetings has just slipped off my shoulders. The West is still here, just as I left it.

THE CUT

The cutting horse approaches the herd as if he were walking on eggs. He moves slowly and deliberately, ears forward, all attention.

The cattle press tightly together on the back fence. They try to hide their heads among their friends, away from the light, trying not to be noticed. Sometimes the horse has to bump the cattle with his shoulder to get in, crowding into the herd and pushing a group of them out. The rules call this a "deep cut."

He drives the group out toward the center of the arena, quietly and carefully. Things can go wrong very quickly in a cutting contest. Some of the cattle begin to file back to the herd. The cutter waits, selects one, and, with a deliberate step this way or that, maneuvers to prevent her from joining the procession.

The rider grips the saddle horn with one hand (a sign of things to come). His other hand has been holding the reins up, showing the horse the way. But with the options now down to one animal, and the horse's ears showing he is committed to it, his hand drops to the horse's neck, and the reins swing loose.

The horse is on his own. It's time to show his stuff.

THE WORK

The modern cutting horse runs parallel to the cow, between her and the herd. He stops and turns quickly to cover her moves. When she fakes, he counters, as in a dance. A good cutting horse may drop his head, putting him on eye level with his quarry. He may move sideways, all legs bent, a cat playing with a mouse.

With fresh cattle being cut for the first time, a skillful horse sometimes can confuse a cow so totally that she will freeze, afraid to move. It's a lucky (and cow-savvy) contestant indeed who finds such a cow.

Other cows will show no respect, closing their eyes, laying back their ears, and squirting back into the herd, no matter what the horse tries.

A rider who thinks the cow has no more play in her, or who thinks he simply may lose her, has the option of leaving her to get a new cow, provided he quits when she is not challenging the horse. She must be standing still or turning away. Quitting when the cow is turning toward you (a "hot quit") costs three points.

You also lose points for scattering the herd, attempting to guide the horse with the reins once the cow is separated, spurring in front of the cinch, losing a cow, or switching cattle.

In most cuttings the scores range from 60 to 74. The highest possible score is 80.

Each contestant gets 2½ minutes to show off his horse. Most of the first 40 or 50 seconds are used for the deep cut. The horse usually will work two or three cows in the remaining time.

JUST FOLLOW THE CROWDS

At Tremonton fairgrounds near the Utah-Idaho border there is a cutting horse contest, but no one ever would know. No mention in any paper, no signs. To find out, you would have to know a cutter or be an NCHA member.

The fairgrounds look deserted: race track empty, grandstand empty, no cars in the parking lot. There are some barns and sheds out back. Oh, look over there. Duallies and horse trailers are parked around one of the barns. And there are a few cars, maybe 10.

Inside the barn, the cutters are gathered. One end is full of guys who look like cowboys. They are exercising horses, cantering around, or just sitting. In the middle of the barn is a small grandstand (not grand at all) with maybe 20 spectators, obviously family and friends. Pokey Richardson spends winters photographing skiers at Park City, but today he's standing with a video camera on an elevated table taping the various cutters. The tapes of all the works are for sale. A TV set is playing earlier action, but no one is watching it, except, I swear, a horse.

The other end of the barn has the action. Two judges are sitting on tables too far apart to let them talk. They take their jobs seriously, spitting tobacco from time to time. And there is the herd, a cutter, and his help. Each cutter gets four helpers, corner men who hold the herd, and "turn-backs" who encourage the cow to even greater action.

One cutter is only about 8 or 10 years old. He is trying to act grown up. He gets a big hand from the usually quiet but always attentive audience. He also gets coaching (step by step) from one of the corner men, probably his father.

We see an old owner, well over 65, whose horse is always shown by a young trainer. He is well liked by the cutters, but going by the conversations, I gather no one ever has seen him ride. Well, today he is talked into riding and showing his own horse, a quickly rigged safety belt holding him on.

His horse, a dandy, drops his head, face into the cow's face, cocks a knee, and starts working. And the old man rides him well.

The crowd begins cheering and applauding. The horse wins his division and the old man smiles. It's almost enough to bring a tear to your eye.

Marvin Thomas rides a mare named Gold San Peppy and wins $500. Any one of the horses in Tremonton easily could outclass the best cutting horse I'd seen those years ago in eastern Washington.

EVEN THE STEAKS ARE JUDGED BY THE CUT

There is a ranch several miles north of Rigby, Idaho, with a dusty arena hidden in a grove of tall cottonwoods. The enclosure is large, suitable for team roping or just about any rodeo event. But a temporary fence forms a pen out of about a quarter of the space.

As always, cutters are galloping their horses in the extra space; other animals are tied to the fence all around. In the pen, someone is showing a horse. I am squatting down, mesmerized, my camera peering through the temporary fence. Two old horsemen standing above me are talking.

"Well, maybe I'll head home and get something done," one says. "I can't stand too much excitement in one day."

"Gosh, you ought to stay for the steaks," the other says. "Last year they were so tender you literally could cut 'em with a plastic fork."

At 6 or 7 that night someone announces that the steaks are served. Some 800 were donated by a local bank, and they are free (with beans). A plastic fork is the only utensil offered — or needed.

NICE CATTLE IN NEPHI

"Cattle? Cattle? You call these good cattle?"

Marvin is remembering a show he judged in Nephi in which the cattle were so good you'd almost have thought they were on your side.

"The cow darts to the left. If your horse is a little slow, she'll stop and wait for him. Your horse is way lost? She'll stop, see the horse is confused, go back in front of him, and wait till he's ready. She'll wiggle her ears to keep his attention.

"Out of 90 horses, only 6 scored a 60. One class was won by a kid who lost a cow. He still got a 74."

SOUR COWS IN SPANISH FORK

I watch Wally Osborne try to quit a determined cow who was about to eat him for lunch. The cow isn't fast or tough, but it is determined to join its mates. It keeps pushing back toward the herd, and nothing Wally or his horse can do makes it turn away.

"Let me off," Wally cries, but his turnback men are already far, far back from the determined cow. She isn't buying; she will not turn away.

Wally's corner helpers see his problem and move in beside him, and they are as noisy as they dare while doing it. The cow still won't quit.

Finally, the turnbacks slip around the action to join Wally. The cow is facing the five horses and five riders, most of whom are waving and making noise, pushing them into the herd. The cow won't turn tail.

The herd scatters and spills around the riders, and Wally quits in disgust. As he rides out, his eyes plead with the judge.

The judge looks at the clipboard on his lap and scribbles something.

"Hot quit," he murmurs under his breath, not looking at Wally. His eyes are moving to the other side of the pen, anticipating the next rider.

HOW CAN YOU PUT A VALUE ON SUCH FUN?

There's a little of the hoss trader in the cutting horse business. A man calls a trainer looking for a horse, something he can cut on, and show, and not embarrass himself too badly doing it.

It just so happens, the trainer allows, that he has just such a horse in his barn, a fine looker, good cow horse, works well. Four thousand dollars.

The man says he is looking for a little more horse than that, but thanks. Trainer promises to keep an eye open.

He waits two weeks. Then he calls the man. "I think I've found the horse you want. Fifteen thousand dollars."

The man takes the bait.

BUSTER AND THE ROUND PENS

In the summer of 1988, a rumor spreads across the western

Rockies that Buster tore down his round pens. Buster is more than just my hero. He practically invented cutting horse training. So everyone was worried. When people heard I was going to Buster's they asked me to find out what Buster was doing, tearing down those round pens.

I felt like a spy.

"Buster, everyone's worried. Why are you tearing down those round pens?"

He laughs. He knows everyone's watching him.

He puts a round pen in a pasture and works the cows in it till they sour. Then he moves it to another pasture with fresh cattle. He always tears them down so he can set them up again at a new place.

We had plenty of time, so Buster explained how he invented the round pen. He said he did it with the help of Shorty Freeman, who worked for him at the time. But first he explained the bubble.

He'd read an article about an experiment in which they put three times as many rats as normal in one area. The rats formed gangs and fought, just like people in the city. Then they experimented with a secretary in an office scene. Someone sits close to her and she feels obligated to talk to them. If he moved her two feet, she goes on with her work. The space close around her was called her "bubble."

Cattle have that bubble, too, Buster says. Get close enough into the bubble and you influence her movement. Too far away and you don't. When the cow first sees a rider the bubble is big. As she gets used to you it gets smaller.

Buster liked to train cutting horses on the big, wide open Texas range.

Someone advised him: "Buster, take your time turning the cow. She can't go anywhere. There's an ocean on each side." When he'd move into the arena he felt cramped and he'd rush his turns.

He read an article about circles. The world, the planets, seasons, cycles. Everything is a circle.

So Buster invented the round pen in which there are no corners to rush things. A horse can rate cattle all day. Buster, and just about every other cutting horse trainer, can take his time. "She can't go anywhere," Buster says. "There's an ocean on each side."

MERKEL, TEXAS

Buster Welch calls himself a cattleman who trains cowhorses.

He collects old saddles and old silver mounted spurs. He also collects cowboy pictures of the old days. The traditional ways are still alive at his place. No one there wears baseball caps, just cowboy hats. He has no mechanical cow.

Visually the center of the place is the cook shack—a kitchen on one side, and a guest room and bath on the other, separated by a breezeway that connects a front porch and a back porch, all screened in. The front porch has chairs so you can watch the yard to see who's coming, and the back porch has chairs so you can watch action in the arena.

In the breezeway, there are three eating tables and benches. Many old saddles line the walls. There are plenty of old photos of historic cow-herding scenes, groups of friends, relatives, old pals, cuttings. There is an old picture of a horse lying down with a man standing on top of him. And a picture of a blindfolded horse jumping a hurdle while he is being ridden bareback by a man.

The place has the atmosphere of a museum except they use it every day. The cook is a Mexican woman, and the meals are so good that Buster's wife, Sheila, seldom needs to use her kitchen in the big house.

For supper, the cook had left rolled wrapped Mexican food in the fridge. Buster warmed them for us in the microwave, a device that seemed incredibly out of place in that scene. When I pointed that out to him he seemed embarrassed. I guessed I wasn't the first to kid him about it.

There is a quote by Calvin Coolidge on the door of the cook shack. Its thrust is that persistence is everything. Luck runs hot and cold and runs out. The gutters are full of educated bums. But, persistence does it all.

The warmup boy told me that the quote is there for lopers who want to be trainers.

EARLY MORNING

The warmup guys start loping at 5 a.m.

In the cook shack guest room, I can hear them, but I look out the window and the sky is pitch black. The arena is lit by a tiny blue light on a pole. It is too dark to shoot color photos. I go back to bed. But someone bangs on my door at 6 and I get up. Buster hands me coffee while I'm in the shower.

I go out to the pen with my cameras but the light meter confirms that it is still too dark to shoot. I am embarrassed at sleeping in so late so I pretend to shoot, the noisy motor drive going bzzzzzt now and then, until the sky begins to glow and the F stops and shutter speed began to cooperate. I have been stalling, waiting for the light, and I think Buster might know

something about cameras because he saves his best horses until the sun is rising behind them.

After the sun is up a bit, we have breakfast. Then we return to the pen. Pretty soon Buster gets a 3-year-old futurity horse and hands me the reins.

"Try her," he says.

After I ride the three year old, I shoot some more pictures, but my heart isn't in it. The sun is getting too high to be pretty, and all the fun is on horseback.

A little later, I ride a 4-year-old mare, and then a horse of Tio Kleberg's that is for sale. Tio had won a large check, maybe $100,000, on this horse a week before. For this one, Buster loans me some chaps and some 100-year-old silver-mounted handmade spurs. The horse is incredible, and I am in heaven.

So I guess the dress code in Buster's arena goes like this: Everyone wears a cowboy hat (no ball caps), and on the good (read: great) horses you wear chaps. Buster tells Sheila to put hers on. Maybe it is the camera. David Holtsford's wife, Nancy, turns back and when the sun goes high she puts on sunglasses. I think Buster makes some disparaging remarks about the glasses.

Later, Dave, a loper, and I follow the cattle down the lane to a pasture. I am riding a 17-year-old gelding that was the first futurity horse Buster ever trained for the King ranch.

During the time I am there, Buster gives me some advice on training horses. Once he quotes the Mormons.

"Marriage isn't any big thing. It's a lot of little things done just right," he says. "Training and riding cutting horses is just like that. Not a big thing, but a lot of little things done right."

And another: Quoting a magazine article he read,

"Old folks don't need much, but what they do need, they need a lot."

Cutting horses have the same needs as old folks.

DAVE THE DIPLOMAT

About noon Dave isn't feeling good. He had looked a little whoozy earlier.

At lunch, Nancy says, "I think we lost Dave." (He'd gone for a nap.)

Buster gets a call from his help, Tom, at another ranch. Then the subject gets around to Dave.

"Dave's a diplomat," I overhear Buster say.

"Nancy's great, just real nice but she can't cook worth a darn. They didn't eat here last night. Should have. Nancy tried to cook. Of course it made Dave sick. He's sick and can't work now. But he's such a diplomat he told Nancy the food was so good he ate too much. We should get him into the government. Get him to talk to those Iranians."

MARION'S GIRL

At night, in the elegant guest room in the rustic cook shack, I read an article by Buster Welch in a 1956 issue of *Cattleman Magazine* titled, "How I Trained Marion's Girl."

I ask Buster about her and he says he figures she was the best he ever saw (and he's seen the best). He gives me a demo of how she'd work a cow that included bugging eyes, low head, and spread fingers. If the cow would crowd her too much she could spring directly back 15 feet and start again.

In about 1956, Buster and Don Dodge (on Poco Lena) were fighting it out for the cutting horse championship. Buster

was leading by a few dollars but it was real close.

Marion Flynt, the horse's owner, told Buster he shouldn't go to that big bunch of California shows. It was Don Dodge country and they liked those fancy reining horse stops. Buster's horses were strictly cowhorses. Marion Flynt thought they should go to the smaller shows in the Northwest instead.

Buster wanted to go to California to face Dodge directly. They needed to beat him there, show that they could, because the last, big shows would be in Texas, where Don Dodge was well known for buying great horses, and Buster was, according to him, just this skinny kid from west Texas.

Well, they went with Buster's plan, and Marion's Girl faced Poco Lena in the California shows. It was close, usually Poco Lena first and Marion's Girl second.

Until one day Buster was turning back for some guy and as time ran out a steer was escaping down the fence in front of the grandstand. Buster caught up with the steer, rated it till they were centered on the stands, and then jumped by it and stopped the horse in a spectacular slide that had those Californians cheering.

After that it still was close but it was Marion's Girl first and Poco Lena second. It stayed that way through the shows in Texas.

HORSES

At a cutting at the J. V. Ferry feed lot, there is discussion about horses and humans. We take our barn-raised horses for granted. Most of our modern cutting horses fit this pampered category. They somehow learn to be tied, led, and handled, almost by osmosis. But a range-raised horse can be all teeth and hooves when cornered by a human.

Some ranch-raised horses in Nevada are so unaccustomed to man that you'd rope them in the morning, saddle them, and ride out. If you came to a gate you got off, opened the gate, got on, and rode the horse through. Then you got off, closed the gate, got on, and rode away.

The horse wouldn't lead.

There was a futurity in Texas where a certain young horse cut a very tough cow to her total confusion. Head to head, noses almost touching, darting back and forth. And when the action stopped, they still were head to head, the horse on his knees ready to pounce any direction, the cow totally confused, the crowd on its feet in ovation.

Later, the horse lost a cow and didn't win. He was headed for the relative obscurity that awaits futurity losers, but writer Tom McGuane heard the story and bought the horse.

What he found was a cutting horse, Lucky Bottom 79, who had been raised and trained by one of those old boys who'd neglected to spend any time with the horse on foot. The horse was freaked by people.

Tom took him to Montana.

One time Marv Thomas had to deliver some mares to McGuane's place. No one was in the house when he arrived, so he poked around a bit before he found Tom had set up his office in the stall with the horse.

He was typing away on a novel in the corner.

A ROOT BEER
Doug and Amy Jordan gave a cutting horse clinic in Cedar City in June, 1989.

Doug is a voice for thoughtful horsemanship in a big money sport that doesn't always have enough time to spend. He speaks for patience, calmness, and thoughtfulness rather than bigger, harsher bits and sharper spurs. He worked for Shorty Freeman and studied with Ray Hunt.

Doug was talking about getting a horse to do what you want, but he spoke in parable.

"If I wanted a root beer and I took out a knife and threatened you, 'Get me a root beer or I'll cut and hurt you', you'd probably walk toward the store till you were out of sight or out of range, and then you'd probably run off. You probably wouldn't come back.

"But if I said to you, 'Gosh it's hot out here. I'm sure thirsty, aren't you?... There's a 7-11 store just down the street...Gosh it's so hot, and I am so thirsty. Boy, a root beer would sure taste good right now. Soft and cold. Cool and refreshing. Delicious.'

"And pretty soon I bet you'd be off and probably go get us a root beer ..."

So a few minutes later I'm sitting in front of the video trailer watching the action in the hot sun. Amy Jordan is on one side and my 24-year-old daughter Anna is on the other. She is living with us again and going to college after being apart for several years. We are bonding. We are having a great time and I'm gently teasing her, talking about the hot sun, the dry dust, and our thirst, and describing the root beers in the cooler sitting over by the fence maybe 40 feet away. After a few minutes of this my ploy works.

Amy Jordan gets up and heads for the cooler, asking what would I like, beer, Pepsi, or root beer?

LEARNING ABOUT COWS

The $2,000 Non-Pro is about to start. They let the cattle in and begin to settle them, forming a herd along the back fence. A rider sifts through them, but they settle against the fence again.

The cutters in this group have won less than $2,000 in NCHA contests before the start of this year. We sit horseback watching the cows we soon will cut.

The cattle are mostly Holsteins, and they tend to stand along the fence facing away from us, their heads hiding together along the panels, tails pointing out. It is sort of a milking time scene.

A professional man we'll call Jack has been in cutting on and off for several years. He is sitting on an expensive mare he bought in Texas, talking about these cattle with his trainer. Which cows would be good to cut, which good to avoid.

There are several of us nearby, all of us about one or two years into this game. Our group contains a writer, a lawyer, and a graphic artist. Reading cattle is not our strong suit. But though we're looking, studying, trying to discern differences, the consensus in our group is that these cows all look alike. So while we are looking, we also are eavesdropping on the trainer and Jack, hoping to learn something.

The trainer talks about the big cow on the left with the black back, and the heifer with the so and so, and that steer with the long head and cropped tail. They are talking and pointing. Our little group is watching the cows but listening intently to them.

And then we can't believe our ears because Jack actually asks, "How do you tell which are the heifers?"

Our heads jerk around in unison to see the reaction of the trainer.

He looks at Jack with the strangest expression, then realizes he wasn't kidding. He looks toward the cattle, all lined up facing the fence. There is a two-second pause before he looks at Jack, sticks out two fingers, and makes a forward thrust with his hand.

We burst out in laughter and jerk our heads in another direction. We are still cracking up when the actual cutting started minutes later.

DOCTOR BILL

There was a Bill Freeman clinic at the Lind Ranch in Marion. Bill rode and trained the current NCHA Futurity champion and is considered one of the very best cutting horse showmen. His dad, Shorty, a cutting legend, is a member of the NCHA Hall of Fame.

This means Bill is a trainer by heredity as well as environment. He was born and bred to cut.

The rule book says the cutter cannot direct any noise at the cattle. Bill gave us a trick of the trade: If the herd is sticky and sour you can cough loudly at them.

Non-pro cutters have non-pro nerves. Bill says a way to calm your nerves and release your tension is to stick out the index finger of the hand you have on the saddle horn. It seems to work, especially when you think of the way it looks to others.

Dick, one of the participants, brought a young bay mare to the clinic. He cut a cow, crossing the pen with her. Then the cow stopped and turned back. The mare stopped and paused, then decided not to turn and jumped ahead.

At that moment I was herd holder in that corner,

about 10 feet from the action.

Dick bumped the bit and reined her back on the cow, but of course the cow was gone.

"Is this something new?" asked Bill Freeman.

Dick said "No" and continued cutting. Pretty soon Bill asked to ride her.

After a few turns with a cow, Bill stopped and pulled the saddle and curiously inspected her back. He tried pressing points on her hip, flank, and back, and we all moved closer to see what was going on.

He hit paydirt on the side of her withers. When he pressed, she cringed in pain.

Dick had brought his problem horse to this famous trainer's clinic to solve her problem only to find it was a physical, not mental, problem. And it looked serious. This was not the diagnosis he expected. We all felt for him.

Conversation and examination led us to believe she had been in an accident two years ago. The more we examined, the more hurt she looked. Slightly crooked spine. One shoulder slightly higher than the other. She apparently had been cutting in pain for some time. We all admired the courage of the little mare, and, though no one mentioned it, we felt Dick's anguish as he must have remembered times he used a jerk on the bit or a spur when she was late in a turn or refused all together. No one mentioned this but we all took glances at his face.

There was a discussion about how a chiropractor might put this mare right. Apparently a good one named Graham routinely visits Bill Freeman's ranch every three months.

Cutting is very strenuous, and a healthy horse invariably is a happy horse.

Then Bill had Dick hold an arm out straight. Bill pulled down on it and had Dick resist the pressure and keep it out straight. Then Dick was told to place his other hand on the horse's hip. Again, Bill pulled down on the arm and Dick could hold it out straight.

They did it again, Dick's other hand now moved to the horse's back. Same results.

Then Bill moved Dick's other hand to the pressure point on the withers, where the mare felt the pain. Bill pulled down on the outstretched arm and Dick is unable to resist. The arm is easily pulled down. Bill says the weak point on the horse absorbed the strength of the human and Dick could no longer hold out against the pressure.

I was amazed, and so was every one else.

THE PIROUETTE

A woman from Idaho, Lynn Campion, wrote a book on training the cutting horse. She said she had a little trouble with her editor. When she described a desired movement as "rolling over the hocks," the editor wanted to change it to "pirouette."

JEEP JUMPING AT THE DOG HOUSE

After Met and Lana's big Cottonwood Canyon Ranch cutting in Antimony, Utah, we decided to meet at the Dog House for a beer before heading home. It is east of Highway 15, about 5 miles before you get to Ruby's Inn at the western entrance to Bryce Canyon.

We got to the Dog House just before sunset and sat on the steps drinking beer and eating nachos, watching the pink clouds, resting from the long day. Our view from the steps was of the gravel parking area and 30 yards of grass that dipped down, curved gradually at the bottom, and rose up to the edge of the highway. Across the road were hills covered with junipers and sage, red rock mountains behind.

When Met and Lana arrived, our group had grown to include their sons Taylor and Ryan, Kathy Thomas, Lew and Evelyn Stevens, and Cha Cha Weller.

And Met told of the jeep jumping.

Apparently when they were on the ranch for days, doing various projects, and in the evenings they would long for running water, flush toilets, and bright lights. They would often go the 20 miles of dirt road south to terrorize the Dog House.

Met can terrorize a place like no one can. He is as famous in Las Vegas as in Antimony, and waitresses, bikers, cutters, and cowboys often are his victims.

Tonight when he pulled up to the Dog House with Lana and the boys, we had seen the old bartender scamper out back to get the owner. Met can mean trouble. It is always good-natured trouble, loud and lovable, but things often get broken and sometimes forewarned is forearmed.

But we were a pretty quiet group for a while, sitting on the steps and kicking our spurs into the dirt.

The jeep jumping started a summer ago on one of those dusty beer-soaked evenings. It started with discussions of what a jeep can or can't do, how it crosses a rock-strewn creek miles from a road, and ends up with a discussion of the topography of the Dog House parking lot—the dip and rise of grass to the highway.

Before long, the bets were placed, and Taylor, Ryan, or Met were spraying gravel all over the Coors Beer sign and

speeding north across the parking lot. Down the dip, up the rise, and airborne across the highway. The idea was to slam on the breaks in midair so that the tires leave rubber marks on the asphalt.

Yes, the West was still wild as recently as last summer. But tonight the jeep was left back at the ranch and we only had the sunset.

MET AND LANA

Daisy came to Lana as a gift from George Stout.

Met and Lana have been friends of George for many years. They used to put on a big cutting together in Las Vegas at the Tropicana Hotel. I guess George noticed Lana watch cuttings with intensity and interest more than most. Because they furnish cattle for several big cuttings and have lots of cutting friends, Lana's been able to catch a ride here and there. She tried to show one of their good ranch horses one summer. So George saw her enthusiasm and gave her Daisy.

It's Saturday morning in mid-winter and we're at Bob Robinson's practicing.

Met's got a new pick up, gold body and black fenders (a buckskin), and he's standing next to it, parked right next to the arena, drinking a beer.

He has a large plastic garbage bag and he has announced to everyone present that it is his day off and he intends to fill it with empty beer cans today. Some of us are helping him.

Bob is a cutting horse trainer, and he has had Daisy for a month or so, and he rides her before Lana. I'm sitting horseback in the corner next to Met. The fence is between us. We're watching and talking about his wife's cutting hobby and her horse. In his soft voice, he is pleased and supportive.

Lana is down the fence a ways, watching carefully. Bob quits a cow, dismounts, and leads Daisy to Lana. They talk intently as they adjust stirrup lengths. As she gets mounted, Met changes to his loudest auction announcer voice and gives her his typical advice. Jim Toomey and Louis Hutchison are up from Las Vegas with horses. Ted has his palomino; Cal is down from Cedar City. Bob's helpers, Nick and Teressa, are there, too. So Met has a nice audience.

"Honey, that mare has been back and forth, fence to fence for about seven years," Met says. "She's been spurred and jerked for a thousand cows. She'll do it, but she's just going through the motions. Just like our sex life, honey."

Lana is used to Met's advice.

"Yeah," she says without missing a beat. "Just cover me up when you're through."

LEW BUYS A SADDLE

In Fort Worth, the Futurity action took place in the Will Rogers Coliseum. Behind the arena was another building, a convention center in which there were lots of booths selling equine paraphernalia. For those of us from Utah, it was like being in a candy store. The first booth we came to after the giant shoe shine stand was M. L. Leddy's, a huge saddle shop and western store. There were displays by most of the famous cutting saddlemakers—Cajun, Calvin Allen, Piland, and, of course, Leddy's.

Lew and I started looking at saddles, one of the larger purchases you can make in the hall short of a truck or trailer. At first glance, all cutting saddles look about the same to laymen: double rig, flat seat, tall horn. But the more we sat on them, swung our feet and grabbed the horn, the more we found subtle differences one to another. The Leddy's were the most expensive, and Lew fell for a slightly used one, only $1,700. We kept looking and went back a few times and finally it wore a tag that said, "Sold, Lew Stevens."

Later, we were watching cutting horses again in the coliseum. We were sitting with Doug Jordan, Kathy Thomas, and Les Tugaw.

"What kind of saddle do you ride?" Lew asked Doug.

"I've got five Morks," he answered. Mork has a display in a trailer between the coliseum and the tuning pen.

At the next cattle change, Lew and I went to see Mork.

In his trailer, Mork was working on a saddle.

"I'll build you one for a base price of $1,500," he said to Lew. "But I'm about three years behind. For another $300 I could expedite it for you. Probably have it in ninety days."

Mork was thoughtful for a few moments. "But then again this one here I'm working on is for Everett Goodwin. He ordered it in December, a year ago at the last Futurity, and he paid the extra $300."

I went back to see the horses working and left my pal with Mork.

When Lew returned, he said he'd ordered another saddle, this time from Mork. He didn't pay the extra $300, and he said he would wait the three years. He said he was going to breed his mare this summer and when her foal is ready to ride, then he'll have his new saddle.

A few hours later, our wives returned from their shopping spree in downtown Fort Worth. The first thing Lew did was to show Evelyn the Leddy saddle with the sold tag, "Very nice," she said. Then, after some hemming and hawing, he took her to the trailer to see the Morks. I didn't join them to witness this, but Lew said later that Evelyn examined the saddles carefully and found an underlying piece of leather that had a slight flaw. With the craftsmanship questioned, Lew withdrew his order. His three-year plan has been sidetracked.

THE FUTURITY

The NCHA Open Futurity has the best cutting horse audience in the world, and the crowd for the semifinals was a good one. They came at 6 p.m. Saturday and stayed till after 1 a.m. watching 60 horses work, cheering and gasping all the way.

The cutting went on and the crowd was with every horse. Mistakes caused gasps. Tough cows caused cheers. Intense horses caused screams. Good work rated applause. The last rider was Tom Lyons, a well known trainer always well mounted and capable of a great work. He sorted through the herd till only one cow was left before him. He put his rein hand down on the horse's neck and the horse trembled with intensity and anticipation, crouched down, eye to eye with the standing cow and then began jumping left and right in front of it like a cat playing with a mouse. The crowd screamed. The cow stared at the dancing horse, and as it jumped to the right she simply trotted past it into the herd.

The cheers turned to a groan and then we heard a new noise. Most people in the crowd stood up and began to make their way out. I was amazed. I watched Tom Lyons cut another cow and put on a great performance but no one else paid any attention. They were leaving. Tom had lost a cow and was not

going into the finals. I guess watching 60 horses cut cows is just about the maximum a crowd can take at one sitting.

THE ATTRACTION

Shooting photos of cutting horses had led me to wonder what a ride on one would be like. A ride led to a lifetime of new questions.

At that point, my interest changed from F-stops and available light to melting into the back of a horse at speed and holding him in the ground with my bottom when he stops. Instead of trying to keep the horse in focus and the cow in the frame, I am trying to keep the cow in focus and my legs out of the horse's way.

Showing a cutting horse has all the challenge of negotiating a mine field. It depends on a lot of finesse and some luck, sometimes at top speed. This, at the outer edge of your tension, with all your adrenaline pumping. And at the same time you'd better relax your legs. The horse can feel everything and he needs to think it's all okay.

Winning a cutting ends with a drive home through the western mountains and valleys, high as an eagle, with Dwight Yokum or Emmylou Harris at full volume.

Losing means a drive home in silence, instant replay over and over in your mind, trying to puzzle just how everything went wrong so quickly.

But what is the attraction? Why do grown men and women put themselves through this?

There are these physical and mental challenges, but there also is an emotional touch with our western heritage in a high tech world.

Maybe the real attraction is the way your fingers smell after handling the reins all day (as opposed, say, to how they smell after a dinner in the sushi bar). It is a subject sometimes discussed by beginning, non-pro cutters. But answers are as elusive as the wind.

THE WIND

One thing about the professionals: They really know how to use their equipment. And we knew it was going to get western when they began to lose their hats.

When the wind blows in Delta, Utah, it really blows. It comes over the mountains, from Nevada, and swoops down, gaining speed as the sagebrush flattens out into hay fields. Dave Hoffman claimed the wind comes all the way from Mexico. He said that now and then he got a whiff of tacos.

Delta is in the middle of a wide flat valley and today a lot of it is in the air. A few miles northwest of Delta is the Cal Ute Feedlot. It seems to raise above the table flat land at about the height of 30 years of cow manure packed and trampled into dust. It's been another summer of drought in Utah, and when the wind hits the feed lot every living thing squints.

Yesterday we arrived at 4 p.m. and the air was calm. At breakfast this morning it still was calm. But the pros started riding Open horses about 10 a.m. and the wind started, too.

The Open horses get the cool morning air and fresh cattle. The horsemen show their horses a time or two and as the day wanes on they depart.

The last class is for beginners. It's really two classes run together in the same herd of sour cattle. One class is for beginning riders learning from a lot of mistakes. Sometimes,

when things get really bad, a 60, the lowest score, can bring home a check. "So and so first, so and so second, and everyone else ties for third." The other class is for trainers trying to get experience for young horses at the risk of disaster at the hands of the cattle who have already been cut several times today and are crazed and wild by now. It's late, and many of the good helpers are gone. The $800 Novice and Novice Novice is a lonely place to cut cows.

The hat rule has long since been thrown out, and everyone is in baseball caps. The sun is low enough to be right in our eyes as I sit watching the 800 begin.

I'm fifth in this herd, normally a pretty good draw. The first four in the herd are novice riders on novice horses and the sour cows are winning. I'm squinting into the wind and angling my head behind the cap brim for protection. The dust is thick and I see back-lit silhouettes of the wildly running cows. Earlier today these cattle would challenge and respect the horses, but now, fueled by the the wind and experience, they just run side to side, then close their eyes and push the hapless horse back into the herd, or dart under his neck. The corner men are helpless and invisible, miserable against the back wall. The herd scatters each time a horse crashes into it. They explode out like a pack of greyhounds. Their mood is in concert with the wind.

Mercifully, the whistle blows on number four. This herd of reruns was deemed settled on this, its last appearance today, but now they are a fired up stampede. There is no chance to win this with skill, but I might be able to help the people who follow me by keeping calm and letting things settle down. Wishful thinking, I suppose, and I blink and pull my cap down and head for the herd.

Remembering some trainer's advice on sour cattle, we enter the center of the herd and split half toward Hal Gunn helping in one corner. I'm hoping to leave two Brahma sprinters back on the fence with the ignored half, but out of the corner of my eye I see them squirt out into the working area. The half I'm pushing slides back tight across me at full speed. I think there is no way they're going into the middle of that arena. I grab the last one, cutting on the run. So much for quiet herd work. In the dust I can barely make out our quarry. We're flying to the right, but I know we're going to be changing direction soon. The situation is ridiculous—hopeless, helpless, and fast.

I feel my right stirrup and sit down and hunch a little. I know what's coming. The cow cuts left, and Doc Baritz plants our 1,180 pounds in the dust as deep as he can. I try to relax and hold him in the ground with my body for as long as I can, probably a trillionth of a second. I try to lift my leg out of his way as he rolls back and turns through himself.

My eyes are burning, dust is everywhere. I can't see my help or anything but the greyhound in front of me. But at least one question is answered: We are relaxed. I know the real fun has started and I can feel myself grinning. I can taste the dirt and manure in my teeth.

Everything is coming up roses in the middle of 40 acres of flying dirt.

ADELITA ROSE
Ian Tyson

The blacks and bays, dapples and greys
Red tailed hawk on summer days
Gravel road winding down to the river
Watch that pony oh goodness knows
He's going to step on your baby toes
Go to sleep and dream of those
Pretty little horses.

Carrying the blood of the steeldust line

52

*This
colt
that
I
ride*

is
my
joy
and
my
pride

so
watch
him
now

you
better
watch
him
now.

Ah,
but
there's

    magic

in
the
horses
feet

in
the
way
they
jump

and
the
way
they
sweep

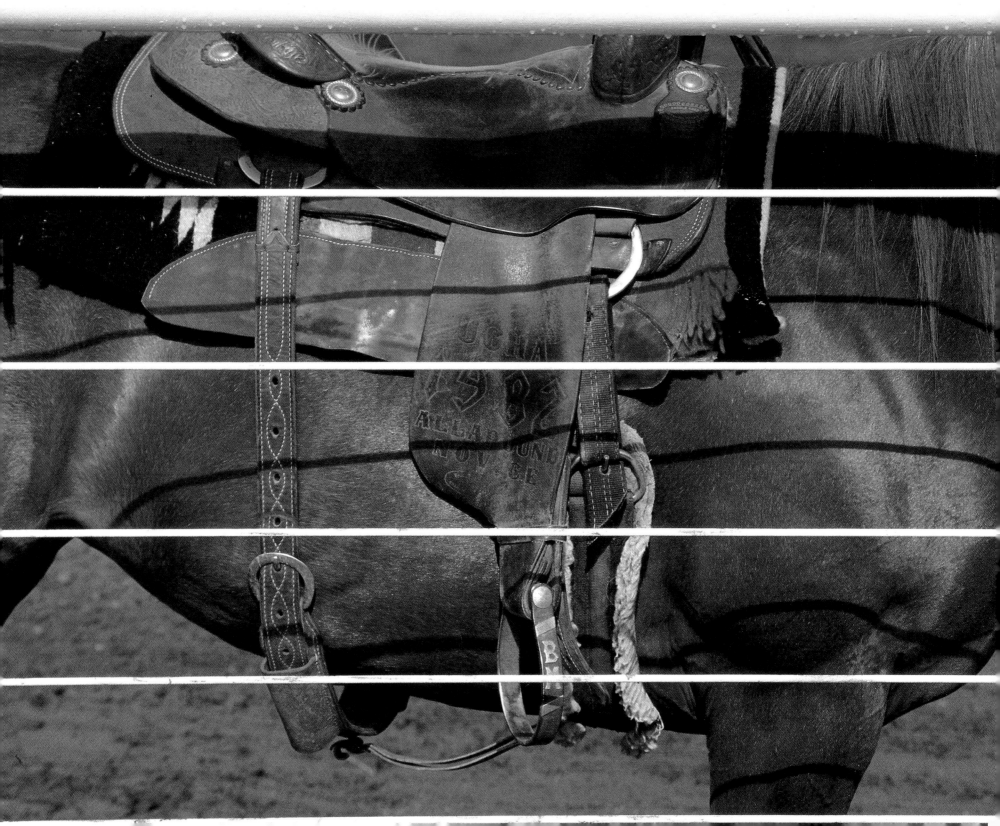

THE CUTTING HORSE

THE CUTTING HORSE

HUB:
CHAMPION
CUTTING
HORSE

Gather Round,
Children, and Listen
... and Remember:
This One
Really Happened

By Robert H. Williams

My name is Hub.
I am a cutting horse,
Or was before Bud Arnett
Turned me out into the cedar brakes
To die of old age.
I fooled Bud there:
I just shrank to a skeleton in a rawhide case
And hung on—
Though the shame and the
lonesomeness nearly killed me.

Then one day—here came a rider over
the rim of the brakes.
I knew at a glance it was Sam Graves
And I let out a wild whinny;

Just couldn't hold it back.
Sam still wore that broad black hat
with high crown
Set square and heavy on his lean head;
His long skinny legs made his feet
appear to sag in the stirrups.
Just sweeping the top of the bunch grass.
I reckon it was the gladdest sight I ever saw.
Sam rubbed me a while, looking me over,
Then took me back the way he had come
Me, wondering all the way
what he was up to.

You see, Sam and I were colts together.
He was sixteen and I was two.
He split two thousand post oak rails
for me
And when I was a little older
He rode me west toward the open range.
We struck up with a bunch of hands
Driving herds west to put together
The new Eight Ranch in King County.
Bud Arnett was the boss.

Right off, Bud traded Sam,
A big, splashy
sixteen-hands-high dun for me!
I was just a medium size blood bay
And Sam was just a dazzled boy
But when Bud threw his saddle on me

And started to ride off
Sam stood there looking
Like a kid about to cry.
Bud then hired Sam
And after we got to the new ranch
He let Sam have me in his string.
That's when they branded the 8
on my left hip;
And we learned the cattle business together.

We loved the open prairie.
It was carpeted with delicious
Curly mesquite grass
Pale green in spring,
Soft gray-brown all winter,
Just one endless sea of it
As far as you wanted to look.

With here and there an island
Blooming purple in summer after
And spicing the clean air
Calves grew fast
And steers got tough and mean—
And not a barbed wire fence
Between here and sundown.
Man, this was horse country!

Sam and I got the hang
Of cutting steers out of the herd.
That's the horse-size job at the roundups.

74

A four- or five-year-old Longhorn
Is the orneriest critter on four feet
When you want to get him
out of the herd.
And calves are still quicker.
They'll twist and spin
And near about run under a horse
Trying to get back into the herd.
I'm close built, light stepping,
And I had plenty of muscle
In the shoulders and hind legs:
I could turn quicker than a long horse;
And I reckon I've always had
A quicker eye, maybe,
Than some horses I could name.

Sam never once threw me off balance.
I always watched the critter's head
And I guess Sam did, too,
The way he stayed right with me.
After all, it was Sam who trained me.
Pretty soon we were cutting out more cows
than anybody else
from any of the other outfits.

And we didn't care how tough they came
Or how long their horns.
Folks got to talking about me—
Hub—Hub—Hub—
That's about all you heard round the

chuckwagons—
As if Sam had nothing to do with the job.

Bud Arnett finally took me away from Sam.
That cut the heart out of Sam—
And me, too.
But Sam was a big man
with the Eight outfit now,
Up next to Bud, himself.
Later on, Sam got himself a ranch
And I didn't see much of him after that.
But Bud was a top cowhand, himself.
He let me work my way
and we made a good team.
He always showed me off at roundups.
Once Gawk Hensley was having trouble
With a tough old rawhide wearing his brand
That kept getting back to the herd.

Gawk was riding a pretty good horse, too.
Finally Bud bet Gawk ten dollars
That I could cut out that steer
with my bridle off!
Well, hell!
Who ever heard of the horse doing the job
all by himself!
Gawk looked at Bud
as if he thought he was crazy
And called his bet.
You can see how that put me on the spot:

I had to deliver.
Cowhands all around saw what was up.
To the man,
they quit work and sat watching
To see if I could do the trick.
We rode about in the herd
Till we jumped that outlaw steer.
When we got on his tail,
Bud leaned forward
And slipped the bridle off my head!
I gasped in spite of myself.
But by that time
I was pushing that critter hard.

We took him on out of the herd
And he twisted
And he turned;
He shot to left
But I cut him off;
He shot to right
And I cut him off again—

The cowboys were yipping
like a pack of coyotes.
Finally that steer
got behind a clump of cedar bushes
And just stood there
Looking me in the eye,
Laughing—
Just daring me to move either way.

Well, I got so mad
I just jumped over the bushes
And bit that varmint on the neck.

I bit him so hard you could hear it pop.
That steer let out a bloody yell
And went right along to the cut
As nice and sweet as a milk cow.
That broke up the roundup for a while,
Everybody was having so much fun
Telling everybody else what I had done.
I guess Gawk Hensley figured
The show was worth the ten bucks.
The old hands never let that trick die
And I became famous
all over the big ranch country.

I thought I was
still going strong enough at twenty
But Bud kept saying
I was slowing down.
That's when he turned me
into the cedar brakes.
Throwed me away
Was the way Sam Graves put it.
I was pretty well stumped
All the time Sam was driving me
up out of the cedar brakes.
Trying to figure out what Sam was up to.
Finally I saw he was taking me

to his ranch.
And when we turned into the horse lot
I found out what he wanted me for.

Some neighbor cowboys
were waiting there to see Sam.
One of them says,
"Where'd you get that stack of bones?"
"That's Hub," says Sam,
And the cowpokes crawled down
off the plank fence
And ganged round me.
Sam said there was going to be
A Cowboy Reunion at Haskell,
July 27 and 28—
That was the year 1898.

Going to be a big horse show—
Roping, bronc riding, cutting and so on.
Said he was aiming
To put me on soaked oats
and prairie hay
And if I mended enough
He was going to ride me
in the cutting event!
Sam said if we won
he was going to split the prize money
With Bud Arnett,
And Bud was going to use his half
To feed me golden oats

the rest of my life!
That put some highlife
into this old carcass.
I guess I started mending right away
For in about ten days
Sam put a saddle on me
And tried me on some figure-eights
And a little galloping and fast stopping.
I was plumb cut down;
Couldn't get started;
Couldn't turn on a half acre;
Just a broken down old nag.
Sam couldn't have been
very happy about me;
Still he was humming a little
As he unsaddled me.

That Cowboy Reunion
was all a fellow heard
From the day Sam went and got me.
You see, folks had fenced
up most of the world
In the past few years.
Since some horse-hater
had invented barbed wire:
There were no more
open-range roundups.
Each ranch crew
rounded up its own cattle,
inside its own fences.

So cattle men didn't get together
twice a year
The way they used to in the old days.
So this Cowboy Reunion was,
you might say,
A statewide open-range roundup.
All the old-timers and rookies too
Were laying off to make that show
And what a show it was going to be:
With the best roping hands
On the best roping horses in the world
Roping for prize money;
The meanest outlaw horses
Bucking the top bronc busters;
The smartest cutting horses,
young and fast,
That's the bunch I would be up against
If Sam rode me.

It wasn't long
Till I began to feel my soaked oats
And Sam was riding me
A little every day.
I still couldn't get going;
Just couldn't pick up my clumsy feet
And put them down
Fast enough for a plow horse.
One day Sam ran up
a bunch of yearlings.
And headed me into the roundup.

Oh man!
Back at work at my old trade!
It felt mighty good, I tell you.
But still, it hurt too—
Me being so slow.
I still could stay right on the tail
Of any old Longhorn
And take him out of the herd,
And I could hold him out,
No matter how foxy.
But when it came to running him
On out yonder to the cut
Where the other cowhands
were waiting for him
And then running back
To cut out the next steer,
Well, any old windbroken nag
On the ranch could beat me.
So Sam wasn't doing
too much humming
And nobody was saying much
About the cutting event
At the forthcoming Cowboy Reunion.

So naturally I was a little surprised
When Sam put a rope on me
And led me off toward Haskell.
We went slow and easy,
Me leading behind the hack,
Taking two days for the trip.

Biggest crowd of people
any cowhorse ever saw.

Sam guessed 15,000.
Folks came from all over Texas
and states around;
Old cowhands I hadn't seen for years;
Voices I hadn't heard
Since the last open-range roundup—
Wisecracking, backslapping,
Tobacco chewing all day.
And the smell of red licker
And sweating cowhands
Took a fellow back to old times.

For two days the bands played
And horses raced
And broncs bucked
And ropers roped.
You never saw
so many bets won and lost.
Then on the morning of the third day
Came the cutting event.
The four hundred-foot-long grandstand
Set up on the bald prairie
Was creaking under its load.
Folks lined the mile-long race track
With wagons, buggies,
and saddle horses.
The band was playing

Horses prancing,
Riders trying to look unconcerned.
Sure 'nuff, Sam threw the saddle on me
And rode me out into the arena!
I felt terrible self-conscious,
My old ribs and hip bones
still showing a little.
Beside those fiery young bucks
I felt old and tacky.
I saw a couple of young cowhands
Looking at me and laughing.
Nobody except a few
of Sam's old cronies
And Bud Arnett and his hands
Paid us any mind.

The man with the megaphone
started talking:
"Ladies and gentlemen ... the cutting
contest!"
Five minutes to each man-and-horse
To see who could cut
The most cows out of the herd.
The winner would get
A hundred and fifty dollars!—
A hundred and fifty dollars!
Both horses and rider would be judged.
There were twelve of us
But everybody was watching
Boley Brown

On a big, prancing six-year-old sorrel.
All the cattlemen knew Boley.
He was a sporty sort of fellow
and a good horseman.
He had earned his big ranch
the hard way.
Nobody begrudged him a dime of it.
His hands used to say
he would pay a poor devil
Twenty dollars for a ten dollar cow
And make the fellow think the cow
was worth the money.
It looked as if everybody
was betting on Boley—
Though every horse there except me
Was young and eager
and fancy looking.
Me—I was twenty-two!

A top hand like Sam Graves
Deserved a fast, young horse.
We drew for places and
The first man called was Boley Brown.
You could hear a dead hush,
Then the crowd roared;
Boley was their man.
The roundup—the herd—
Was made up
Of a bunch of spayed heifers
Fresh from the range country,

Tough and quick and wiley as foxes.
Boley rode his big sorrel
Into the roundup
And came ripping out
Pushing out one of those heifers.
She zigged and she zagged
But Boley's horse
Outzigged and outzagged her.
He took her on out to the cut,
And then he flew back for the next one.
He got on the tail of another heifer
And took her right on out
The same as before.
I hadn't seen work that smooth
In many a day.
Three—four—five—six—
Boley was making time.
He was on a mighty good horse.
But the seventh heifer
Turned and twisted,
Lunged to left
Spun to right,
Turned head-on to that big sorrel:
Then she caught him—
Or maybe Boley—
Off balance for a split second
And shot back into the herd.
That would cost Boley.
But mighty quick that big sorrel
Came out of the herd

With another rawhide heifer;
Then still another.
Eight in five minutes.
Not counting the one he lost.
Any horse that beat that record
Would have to have wings.
I did think I might have got
Started out of the herd a little quicker—
But maybe I was thinking back
a few years.

The second man let the first heifer
outsmart him.
His horse wasn't in the running.
Then the megaphone voice called us:
"Sam Graves riding Old Hub."
A lot of folks scattered here and there
Must have recognized the names
For they stood up in little knots
Looking with their mouths open,
Just to watch this ghost walk, I reckon.
Straight for the roundup we galloped.
I knew and Sam knew our one chance
Was to lose not a step, not a second
In getting the beasts on their way.
We picked up a lean, brindle critter;
You could see she was scared half to death;
But that only made her the wilder.
She twisted to left but we blocked her;
She shot back to right but we beat her;

It was risky to crowd her
But we couldn't just stand there—
So we bluffed her on out to the cut.
We heard the crowd
yelling and whooping,
But I crept back as slow as a snail!
We cut out a second wild heifer and
worked her on out to the cut;
Then we ran out the third, and another—
We were working as smooth as a shuttle
And the grandstand
was buzzing like bees.
Number five was swift and light-footed;
She turned and she faced me head-on;
When I rushed her
she swung toward my left side
But I just stuck out a front foot.
I had used that old trick
at the roundups
But you never saw such a wild crowd.
I used it again on the sixth one;
Our seventh we bluffed like the first.
We needed one more to tie Boley
But the time surely was running out.
As we galloped back
straight for the roundup
The crowd rose up and went silent
And I was a-lather all over,
But Sam sat as light as a cloud.
Yes, we did it: we jumped still another;

I pushed her right out with my nose.
The pistol shot ended my fever,
But we had number eight at the close.

Well, that just about tells the story.
One other horse cut out eight heifers
But the judges were unanimous:
It was Sam Graves and Old Hub
for the money.
They said we had done
The best footwork and headwork.
The stands sounded like a cyclone
Ripping the roof off a barn.
Sam just sat there
wearing a sheepish smile.
I reckon he didn't dare try to speak;
And that's the way I felt, too.
When the storm began to quiet down
Harry Dougherty, boss of the reunion,
Asked us to put on a little act
he had heard about:
Cut out a heifer, me without my bridle.
So we did, just for fun of course.
Sam rode me into the herd,
Slipped off my bridle
And we ran a heifer out to the cut.
Then—just for fun, of course—
We galloped back and cut out another,
It was a good day,
One of the best Sam and I ever had.

For both the inspiration and information for this prose-poem about Hub, the famous cutting horse of the 1880s and 1890s, I am indebted to the book The Big Ranch Country, *Chapter 2, by my brother, J.W. Williams of Wichita Falls, Texas. J.W. had the good fortune to interview Sam Graves at his ranch in the 1940s to get the personal account of the story of Hub. Mr. Graves, then in his eighties and a breeder of fine horses, still loved Hub and rated him the best cutting horse he had ever known. He had clippings from the Haskell Free Press of July 30, 1898, showing a picture of him and Hub and verifying the story published in the newspaper.* The Big Ranch Country *was originally published by Terry Brothers, Wichita Falls in 1954, and reprinted by Nortex Press in 1971.*

Sam Graves on Hub.

79

THE STEELDUST LINE
Ian Tyson

Left early Tuesday morning
Hit the border right at 10
The vet said where you headed son
Said Vegas sir and then
We hooked her through Montana
Made good time—roads were bare
By nite fall we're in Dillon
Ten below and cold down there.

Fed the partners in the morning
We were Nevada bound
Down the steep Monida Pass
Ford runnin' like a hound
Across the foggy flat lands
Of southern Idaho
Turned south into the sagebrush hills
And the cowtown of Elko.

CHORUS
Carrying the blood of the steeldust line
Carrying the blood of the steeldust line
Looking for silver, looking for gold
Looking for the big pay day
I know my silent partners
Stand behind me all the way.

Dick Jones had good fresh cattle
A nice dry building, too
So we went to cutting cattle
And in four days time we knew
The partners were as ready as they
Were a'goin to be
So we left in a blizzard
On Monday morning
And all that I could see
Were the taillights of a trucker
Driving into the blizzard's jaw
But that trucker never weakened
All the way to Tonapah
We dropped down on the desert
We left the storm behind
Four more hours we're in Vegas
Traffic and freeway signs.

CHORUS

Well, I found the Tropicana
Then I found the draw
The whole damn Doc Bar dynasty
Was posted on the wall
With Gunsmokes and Quixotes
Col Freckles, too—Little Peppys,
Mr. San Peppy's,
The cutting horse who's who.

Put the splint boots on the partner
Pulled my latigo up tight
Rode into the herd
And cut my first cow out just right
Drove out to the middle
Turned my partner free
Ed and Lindy in the corners
They were a'takin' care of me.

CHORUS

When the buzzer sounded
I'd got my partner shown
Picked up a check for my 217
Headed north back home
But look for me next winter
I'll be back for sure
For I'm a carrier of the cuttin' disease
For which there is no cure.

*Saddle
them
ponies,*

*open
the
gate*

*gather
them
cattle
'cause*

*supper
can
wait*

Put
the
splint
boots
on
the
partner

Pulled
my
latigo
up
tight

rode   *turned*
into   *my*
the   *partner*
herd   *Drove out to the middle*   *free …*

and
cut
my
first
cow
out
just
right.

*Well,
I
found
the
Tropicana*

*then
I
found
the
draw.*

The whole damn Doc Bar dynasty

was
posted
on
the
wall.

*Funny
thing
about
this
cuttin'
game.*

*A
man
gets
hooked*

*he's
never
the
same.*

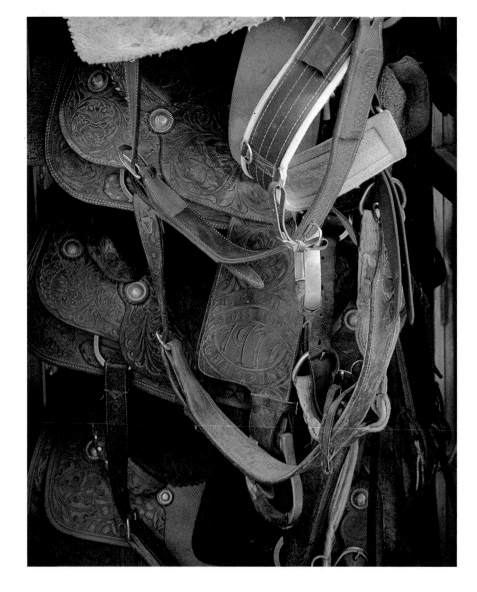

COMPETITIVE
FIRES
From Jackpot Cuttings to
$1 Million NCHA Purses

By *Patrick Steenberge*

Open range cutting competitions grew as the 20th Century began, with bragging rights and side bets going to the owner of the best horse. The ranch manager and top hand always rode the quickest, most agile cutting horse. Although the big ranches were fenced, the cutting horse still retained his exalted position.

Impromptu cuttings and outdoor arena contests flourished. Many cowboy gatherings were highlighted by the cutting competition. Rules and prizes varied widely, but the uncanny ability of the cutting horse to separate single calves from the herd always was the stated goal.

Jackpot cutting became regular events on the ranches of the Southwest and in the Fort Worth Stockyards, where cutting horses were an integral part of the daily cattle operations. As the competition grew in popularity, winning became a matter of pride, which honed a horse and its rider together as a team.

Affection between a cowboy and his cutting horse was something special. Old-timers say a cowboy would sooner "fight for his horse before he would his brother."

That pride gave cutting the momentum to propel the competition to further refinement and widespread acceptance. In keeping with that development, the first known indoor cutting contest was held March 14, 1908 in conjunction with the National Feeders and Breeders Livestock Show, the forerunner of the Southwestern Exposition and Fat Stock Show. The Saturday night contest was the closing-day feature. Bob Schertz rode away with the $50 first prize on a horse named "Ned."

By 1918, the Fort Worth Fat Stock Show featured 27 horses in its annual cutting competition. The purse totalled $2,400 that year, and John C. Crouch of Lometa, Texas, won the event on a small black horse named "Buck." The horse was declared "the best cutting horse ever shown in Fort Worth" by *The Daily Livestock Reporter*.

Through the years, the competitive format has changed with the ongoing refinement of the sport. Before the organization of the National Cutting Horse Association, rules at all the ranch and exposition contests varied. At times, participants were given five minutes to cut as many calves as possible and drive them one at a time to a given point in the arena. Other events required contestants to draw a color before competing, then cut a calf marked with the same color.

Some contests were judged by the number of calves a horse and rider could drive past a white line painted in the arena, then hold them there. Still other competitions required contestants to drive a single steer into a small pen through a blind door. The difficulty involved in this procedure truly tested the skill of both the horse and the rider. One cowboy said it was "like pouring a steer through a crack in the floor."

When organizers began to plan for official recognition of cutting as a sporting event, Fern Sawyer of Nogal, New Mexico, and Grady Blue of Palo Pinto, Texas, approached the "Turtles Association" to request that cutting be recognized independently as a rodeo event. The group that today is known as the Professional Rodeo Cowboys Association (PRCA), turned the request down then, feeling they had too many events already.

In answer to the need to standardize competition rules and provide for cutting's recognition as an independent sporting event, the National Cutting Horse Association was formed in 1946. The original 13 members who got together that day in Fort Worth lit the fuse for the explosion that followed subsequent decades.

The founders included: Milt Bennett, Emry Birdwell, Grady Blue, Eddie Caldwell, Ray Smyth, Rich White, A.B. Edsal, R.C. Edsal, Don Flint, George Glascock, Volney Hildreth, Margaret Montgomery, and Fern Sawyer.

The group's first organizational meeting was held amid the tents and hay bales of the 1946 Fort Worth Exposition and Fat Stock Show, with a dozen or so ranchers in attendance. The organization originally was to be called the Southwestern Cutting Horse Association, but the name was revised at the second meeting to the National Cutting Horse Association.

The group subsequently elected Ray Smyth of Aledo, Texas, to serve as the first president of the NCHA. Smyth's grain mill in Aledo served as the group's first headquarters. Aledo's lawyer, Raymond Buck, drew up the legal work for the

NCHA in exchange for some help working cattle on his ranch outside of town.

After its organization, enthusiasm in the NCHA spread quickly throughout the United States, according to Smyth, who saw membership nearly double the first two years. "When the first year was over, we had members in twelve or thirteen states," Smyth said. "By the time the second year ended, about twenty states were represented."

Along with the growth in individual membership, the NCHA began attracting a diversity of groups as affiliate members. The first to join in those early years was the Parker County Sheriff's Posse of Weatherford, Texas.

Shortly after formation of the NCHA, the first approved contest was held in the fall of 1946 at Everett Colborn's ranch in Dublin, Texas. From that first competition, cutting horse contests have grown and matured dramatically over the years.

Starting with that first official NCHA cutting horse contest in Dublin, the only event that the NCHA was concerned with was "open" cutting (an open cutting is one in which any horse can enter regardless of age, sex or breed).

During the 1950s, the NCHA experienced steady growth, which included keeping money-winning records of novice horses. The Tournament of Champions, which was the first attempt at a qualifying event, also began in the 1950s. Horses earned the right to be in the tournament through their yearly earnings in the open class only. These horses worked six times (go-rounds) in the tournament, with 10% of the money paid in each round and 40% paid for the total. It created a great deal of excitement, leading the way for future major NCHA events.

In the early 1960s, one of the NCHA members suggested that the Association try a Futurity for 3-year-old cutting horses. The first NCHA Futurity was held in Sweetwater, Texas in November, 1962. A total of 36 horses competed for $18,375 in prize money. This event had a marked influence on the future of the National Cutting Horse Association and its current success. The Futurity has established new records each year and has become the richest annual indoor horse event in the world.

In 1962, the National Cutting Horse Association also held its first independent World Championship Finals at the Thunderbird Hotel in Las Vegas, Nevada. An added purse for the finals of $5,000 and a total purse of $16,800 was the largest purse ever offered in a cutting horse contest. Forty-nine horses entered the contest in the hopes of taking home part of the purse and winning the NCHA World Champion Cutting Horse title because this show would signify the official end of the NCHA point year. As the scope of the NCHA changed, the Finals also included a "non-professional" division, which started in 1964, with an added purse of $1,500.

The institution of a non-professional class was a major breakthrough in NCHA policy because it allowed men and women who made their living away from cutting to compete against others with similar time constraints. The non-pro class now is a part of every NCHA-approved cutting horse contest. In many cases, it outdraws the open class for entries.

According to NCHA rules, a non-professional can win money in cutting horse events. However, he or she must own the horse being ridden. Non-pros cannot receive remuneration of any kind for training cutting horses.

The need for this class was a direct result of the changing makeup of the membership of the Association. The ever-growing number of cutting horse enthusiasts included those whose business restricted their activity to a weekend or hobby basis. Those people needed a place to show their horses against other people in similar situations. Prior to this time, NCHA approval only had been granted to shows open to the world.

Also included in the changes of 1964 was the establishment of a Youth Division. Approved youth contests aimed at the horse-minded American youth for both boys and girls were partially the result of successful NCHA youth programs as well as those of various Agricultural Extension Services and the National High School Rodeo Association Finals. The Association felt that it was important to establish a youth program under the highest standards and to reward those meeting minimum requirements with suitable recognition concerning horsemanship and sportsmanship.

The National Cutting Horse Association soon found out that it could adapt to almost any problem and was ready to take on new areas. The first of these was the NCHA Derby for 4-year-old horses, which began in 1970. Before that little or no money was available for 4-year-old cutting horses. Thus, many horses were dropped from training after The Futurity.

The Derby originally was held in Albuquerque, but it was found that this was too far from the center of the horse population. It then was moved to Waco, Texas, where it experienced solid growth. In 1979, the Derby had 129 entries competing for a total of $72,500 as compared to 50 horses in 1970 competing for $18,237. In 1990, the NCHA Derby, now located in Fort Worth, had 277 entries vying for a total purse of $319,000. Because a non-professional division had been added, riders had good reason to continue training their 4-year-old cutting horses after The Futurity, just like the professional trainers. The lure was a healthy purse.

The NCHA also approved the division of the United States and Canada into championship areas to better accommodate the number of weekend and hobby cutting horses. The division began to take shape in 1976 and has been growing ever since. This reduced the number of miles a contestant had to haul his horse in order to be competitive with other horses, because only the points earned within the horse's home area counted toward year-end awards. In addition to competing for their individual area championship, they also competed for the right to enter the NCHA Area Champions Work-off. This was accomplished by finishing the point year as one of the top 10 horses in their home area. The work-off experienced reasonable growth through the years while it was rotated among several locations. Then, Jackson, Mississippi became home.

With an interested host city, the addition of Chevrolet as a corporate sponsor, and continued growth at the grass-roots level, the event now has attained major status. The renamed National Championships now is the largest annual NCHA event, with more than 700 entries representing 35 states and Canada.

While the 1960s and 1970s were a period of rule changes and new events, the 1980s saw a meteoric growth in the sport throughout the world.

The first $1 million purse in cutting was offered at the 1982 NCHA World Championship Futurity. The $2 million mark was achieved in 1985 at the same show.

From the original hopes of 50 members in 1946, NCHA membership swelled to some 15,000 in 1985. One strong attraction of cutting is that a competitor can win money at this sport. Many cutters are drawn to an equine event where some of the investment in the horse, tack, trailer, or training can be recouped in the arena. More than $17,000,000 in prize money is distributed annually in cutting events.

The 1980s also saw powerful upswings in both the "weekend" shows and the "major" limited age events.

More than 120 cutting clubs sprang up in the U.S., Canada, and seven foreign countries. These affiliates are the backbone of the NCHA, organizing and operating some 1,600 contests annually that attract 150,000 entries.

Most cutters belong to their local affiliate as well as the national organization. They all are linked by a love of the sport, competing under the same rules with approved judges. The NCHA has worked tirelessly to ensure that each horse and rider that enters the herd has an equal opportunity to win.

There now are classes for every level of expertise and experience on the local level. These include:

Open: The class is open to any horse, regardless of age, breeding, or sex, and may be ridden by any person who is an NCHA member.

Non-Professional: Open to any rider who holds a valid Non-Pro card and is an NCHA member. The horse may be any age or sex, and must be owned by the rider or his or her immediate family.

$20,000 Limit Amateur: Limited to NCHA Non-Professional card holders whose lifetime earnings in NCHA

Approved Non-Professional Contests equal less than $20,000.

a. No person may compete in this class who has ridden, trained, or assisted in training horses or horse riders for remuneration directly or indirectly, nor may such a person's spouse, relative of either living in the same household, or minor children. Any person who received pay to work on the premises of a horse training operation shall also be ineligible.

$10,000 Non-Pro: Limited to NCHA Non-Professional card holders whose lifetime earnings in NCHA Approved Non-Professional contests equal less than $10,000.

$3,000 Limit Novice: Open to all horses having lifetime earnings of $3,000 or less as determined from the records of the National Cutting Horse Association. (Limited age event earnings do not affect novice eligibility.)

$2,000 Limit Rider (Any Horse): Open to anyone whose lifetime earnings equal less than $2,000. A contestant may compete on any horse regardless of ownership.

$1,500 Limit Novice: Open to all horses having lifetime earnings of $1,500 or less as determined from the records of the National Cutting Horse Association.

Open Gelding: Open to any gelded horse.

Youth: Open to any person 18 years or younger.

As for the major events, the NCHA has added the Super Stakes and Breeders Cutting for 4-year-olds, Classic for 5-year-olds, and Challenge for 6-year-old horses. Each of these shows now are one to two weeks long, drawing upwards of 500 horses competing for millions of dollars. They each feature events that are supported by corporate sponsors, coveted by host cities, and covered by regional and national media.

The NCHA Futurity has continued to expand to a pre-eminent position in the cutting horse sport. Each December, sellout crowds of knowledgeable spectators jam the legendary Will Rogers Coliseum in Fort Worth for The Futurity Finals. The Futurity draws an eclectic mix of horse lovers from around the world. They come to see these 3-year-olds compete for the first time ever, to see who will be the stars of tomorrow.

They also are drawn by the myriad of horse sales, social functions, parties, and the annual NCHA convention. It is the one time each year when old friends and new acquaintances gather and discuss the sport they all love, while watching the very best in the world compete in this classic confrontation between horse and cow.

The days of rugged range challenges are gone, but the spirit of the Old West remains a guiding force of the competition. Then, as now, the National Cutting Horse Association remains committed to its original goals—the preservation of the cutting horse's western heritage and the continuing refinement of its performance in the arena.

NON PRO SONG

Ian Tyson

Every evening on the interstate
Stop and go traffic he can hardly wait
To turn on the gravel
Leave the downtown core behind.
Technology was going to set us free
That ain't the way it turned out to be
A little bit of leisure is
Harder and harder to find
He hits the gravel with some relief
He's older now and it's his belief
He maybe should have been just
A cowboy on the land
So saddle them ponies, open the gate,
Gather them cattle 'cause supper can wait
It's the day in the life
Of a non-pro cuttin' horse man.

BRIDGE

This could be the year he puts it all together
This could be the year he finally gets it right
With a little luck and a lot of concentration
He'll be riding in the finals
On a Fort Worth Saturday nite.

(Y'know its a)
Funny thing about this cuttin' game
A man gets hooked he's never the same
All he wants to do is ride and hunt a cow
So he'd better have an understanding wife
And keep it all together in his business life
If he wants to be cuttin' a couple of years from now
Ah, but there is magic in the horses' feet
In the way they jump and the way they sweep
It's an addiction, not that hard to understand
So, saddle them ponies, open the gate,
Gather them cattle 'cause supper can wait
It's just a day in the life
Of a non-pro cuttin' horse man.

EYES
ON THE
COW

Learning

to Cut:

A Lesson

From Leon

By Randy Witte

I've become very intrigued with cutting, and last fall I found out firsthand why this sport is rapidly gaining in popularity. I'd never been on a cutting horse before, but thanks to Leon Harrel, the 1987 NCHA Futurity champion rider, I got to do some cutting at his ranch just outside of Kerrville, Texas.

I met up with Leon at a small weekend cutting, an NCHA contest held right there at Kerrville. Leon was showing several cutting horses. He had plenty of good help, warming up horses, but didn't want to leave me standing at the rail, so, before long, I was horseback with the others in the warm-up pen, doing a lot of walking and trotting, and some loping. Leon likes to warm them up long and slow, and his horses are invariably relaxed and willing athletes who look like they really enjoy their work.

At the cutting, I met the legendary Buster Welch, and also shook hands with Jim Reno, NCHA president. I told Jim I was pleased to meet him, and Leon shot back, "Don't be so sure; you haven't known him as long as I have." Then he laughed, and Jim just shook his head and grinned. In cutting horse circles, I discovered, Leon Harrel has a reputation for subtle, homespun humor, which he dispenses freely.

In the days ahead, I was totally immersed in cutting. I watched Leon working young horses he has in training. He had about 40 horses at the ranch at the time, and they all looked like they came from the same mold—14.3 hands, great conformation and muscling, and a pretty head on every one of them. We talked for hours about cutting horses—how to ride them, train them, keep them healthy.

Toward the end of my stay with Leon, I was getting pretty cranked up about the sport, and was just itching to find out for myself exactly what it felt like to ride a horse that can do all that fancy footwork. I finally popped the question.

"You want to cut a cow?" he said. "I've got a nice little palomino mare you'll really like."

I'd already seen her in a stall just outside Leon's office, at the indoor arena. Leon had got her in last spring as a green-broke three-year-old, and in the months since then she had a real handle put on her, and was now a solid horse.

Leon helped me set the stirrups, a very precise adjustment in cutting, I discovered. I warmed up the mare while Leon and his crew brought in the cattle, and tried to remember everything Leon had told me about riding a cutter.

"A person wants to stay relaxed in his hips and lower back," he'd said. "We call that the cutter's slump. Sit slightly off the cantle, and relax your back. As the horse moves, you'll take most of the shock from the stops and turns in your back.

"In a stop, you'll keep from going forward by pushing on the saddle horn. When the horse gets up to go after that cow, you'll pull on the horn. That's how you maintain that posture."

I made my first cut, trying to do it just the way Leon had explained, going deep in the herd and cutting for "shape," letting the cattle flow back around on either side and finally deciding on a cow. I dropped my rein hand to the mare's neck, and saw her head disappear. Suddenly, we were moving left, then right, then back to the left. I was pushing and pulling on the horn, and the gravity force in those sudden stops and turns told me what it must feel like to ride in a high-performance airplane. The mare was doing it all, and I remembered something else Leon had said:

"You're watching what happens, but you're not supposed to get directly involved. You're the silent partner, letting the horse do what he has been trained to do. Your goal is to not interfere with his movements. If he's doing it right, stay out of his way and let him do it. Don't anticipate the horse's moves or the cow's moves—if you do, you'll make a mistake."

I cut a couple more cows that afternoon, and at one point I found we were engaged in an equine-bovine standoff. Cow and horse stood still, eyeing one another, the cow trying to figure which way to try next, the horse daring her to move. I felt a big grin on my face, and glanced down to admire that great little palomino mare. The next instant I was hiked out of the saddle, off to the side, and I raised my hand to stop.

That's when I remembered something else Leon had said: "Whatever you do, don't take your eyes off the cow."

THE FUTURITY
Ian Tyson

This colt that I ride is my joy and my pride
So watch him now—you better watch him now
This little stud's got the heart and the blood
So watch him now—you better watch him now
Cause I've had this dream forever it seems
And it's time now to make it come true.
If everything gets right on this clear Fort Worth night
You will see what this pony can do.

If everything gets right on this clear Fort Worth night

You will see what this pony can do.

APPENDIX

NCHA HALL OF FAME MEMBERS

Inasmuch as certain individuals, through their own efforts and those of the horses they raise, make over a period of time an outstanding and unusual contribution to the NCHA's basic purpose of the public exhibition and constant promotion of the Cutting Horse, it is hereby agreed: that an NCHA Members Hall of Fame be created and perpetuated to honor the individuals who have exhibited the characteristics set out herein: A high moral character, good sportsmanship, fairness, extraordinary contribution or commitment to the Cutting Horses in the NCHA, and an exemplary contribution of time, effort and interest in the NCHA and its basic endeavors.

Ray Smyth (deceased), Aledo, Texas
Don Gould, Katy, Texas
Robert "Bob" Burton (deceased), Arlington, Texas
Phillip Williams (deceased), Tokio, Texas
George Glascock, Cresson, Texas
Marion Flynt (deceased), Midland, Texas
Tom B. Saunders (deceased), Fort Worth, Texas
Volney Hildreth (deceased), Fort Worth, Texas
Grady Blue (deceased), Palo Pinto, Texas
Emry Birdwell, Palo Pinto, Texas
Fern Sawyer, Nogal, New Mexico
Don Carr, Burleson, Texas

C.P. Honeycutt, Maricopa, Arizona
Zack T. Wood, Jr., Fort Worth, Texas
Harry J. Guffee, Franklin, Tennessee
Douglas B. Mitchell (deceased), Fort Worth, Texas
Buster Welch, Sweetwater, Texas
Don Dodge, Paso Robles, California
J.M. "Shorty" Freeman, Era, Texas
Matlock Rose, Aubrey, Texas
L.M. "Pat" Patterson, Tecumseh, Oklahoma
Col. Ike Hamilton, West Monroe, Louisiana
Dale Wilkinson, Waynesboro, Georgia

NCHA HALL OF FAME HORSES

To give the cutting horse greater recognition, an NCHA Hall of Fame has been established to credit famous cutting horses. To be placed in the Hall of Fame, a horse must win $35,000* in NCHA Open Championship Contests. Upon winning the $35,000* a Gold Certificate will be issued to the owner of the horse and a plaque with the horse's and owner's name will be placed on the walls of the NCHA office. Recipients of the NCHA Hall of Fame Awards have also received the Silver and Bronze Awards.

*1980—Amended to $50,000
*1981—Amended to $100,000
*1985—Amended to $150,000

Alice Star - Houston Clinton, Burnett, Texas
Annie Glo - Bridget May, Wichita Falls, Texas
Ball O'Flash - Connie Sue Ashcraft, Decatur, Texas
Booger Red - Manual Kulwin, Chicago, Illinois
Chickasha Dan - Casey Cantrell, Nara Visa, New Mexico
Chico Gann - Andy Nored, Bowie, Texas
Delta - George Price, Fairview, Tennessee
Doc N Willy - Edwin B. Jones, Redding, California
Doc Wilson - Dr. Elvin D. Blackwell, D.C., Dallas, Texas
Doc's Oak - Tom Lyons, Phoenix, Arizona
Doc's Playmate - Leon Harrel, Helm, California
Doc's Starlight - Lee Holsey, Corsicana, Texas
Dolly Brian - R.L. "Sonny" Chance, Houston, Texas
Dry Doc - M.L. Chartier, Fairhaven, Michigan
Fizzabar - Don Dodge, Marysville, California
Gandy's Time - Jim Lee, Iowa Park, Texas
Handle Bar Doc - Jim Eddings, Athens, Texas
Heart 109 - Sonny Braman, Shaker Heights, Ohio
Hollywood Cat - Louis Dorfman, Dallas, Texas
Hollywood Lin - David and Jane Gage, Wichita Falls, Texas
Hoppen - Del Jay Associates, Ohio and Wichita Falls, Texas
Jazzote - George W. Glover, Bay City, Texas
Jose Uno - John Bradford, Gadsden, Alabama
Kingstream - David Gage, Wichita Falls, Texas
Little Tom W - Don Strain, White River, South Dakota
Marbo McCue - Jimmie Orrell, Monticello, Arkansas
Marion's Girl - Marion Flynt, Midland Texas
Miss Nancy Bailey - Bob Burton, Arlington, Texas
Miss Elite - Gabe McCall, Aurora, Colorado
Montana Doc - Gene Suiter, Los Olivos, California
Mr. Holey Sox - J.T. Fisher, Bridgeport, Texas
Mr. San Peppy - Agnew and Welch, Lessee; King Ranch, Kingsville, Texas
Patty Conger - E.H. Mooers, Richmond, Virginia
Peponita - Matlock and Carol Rose, Gainesville, Texas
Peppy San - Douglas Lake Cattle Company, Ltd., Douglas Lake, B.C., Canada
Peppy San Badger - King Ranch, Kingsville, Texas
Poco Lena - Skipper Cattle Company, Longview, Texas
Poco Mona - Orange Rice Milling Company, Orange, Texas
Poco Stampede - Mrs. G.F. Rhodes, Abilene, Texas
Royal Chess - Clyde Bauer, Victoria, Texas
Royal Hank - Larry Shearin, Creve Coeur, Missouri
Sandhill Charlie - Slim Trent, Fallon, Nevada
Senor George - Senor George Enterprises, Mt. Clemons, Michigan
Slats Dawson - George J. Pardi, Uvalde, Texas
Snipper W - Primo Stables, Victoria, Texas
Stardust Desire - Douglas Lake Cattle Company, Ltd., Douglas Lake, B.C., Canada
Snappy Dun - Edgar R. Brown, Fort

137

Pierce, Florida
Sugar Vaquero - Sandy Currie and
   Glendon Johnson's Brazos Bend
Ranch, Houston, Texas
Swen Miss 16 - L.M. White,
   Chiefland, Florida
Tenino San - Bob and Patsy Brooks,
   Whitesboro, Texas
Vegas Boy - Walt Gardner, Las Vegas,
   Nevada

NCHA HALL OF FAME RIDERS

The Riders Hall of Fame honors those
riders who have distinguished
themselves in the cutting horse
contest arena by riding outstanding
horses in NCHA programs and
NCHA sponsored limited age events.

Philip Williams (deceased), Tokio, Texas
Sonny Perry (deceased), Ward, Texas
Buster Welch, Sweetwater, Texas
Matlock Rose, Aubrey, Texas
Shorty Freeman,(deceased), Era, Texas
Tom Lyons, Grandview, Texas
Leon Harrel, Kerrville, Texas
Bill Freeman, Rosston, Texas
Joe Heim, Thackerville, Oklahoma
Don Dodge, San Miguel, California
B.A. Skipper (deceased), Longview,
   Texas
Jack Newton, Krum, Texas
Gene Suiter, Los Olivos, California
Jim Lee, Iowa Park, Texas
Stanley Bush, Mason, Texas
J.T. Fisher, Moultrie, Georgia
John Carter, Clermont, Florida
Keith Barnett, Fulshear, Texas
Leroy Ashcraft, Decatur, Texas
Curly Tully, Goldthwaite, Texas
Pat Patterson, Tecumseh, Oklahoma
Terry Riddle, Wynnewood, Oklahoma
Larry Reeder, Stephenville, Texas

NCHA HALL OF FAME
NON-PROFESSIONALS

To give the Non-Professional rider
greater recognition, an NCHA Hall
of Fame has been established. To be
placed in the Hall of Fame, a rider
must win $35,000* in NCHA
Championship Non-Professional
Contests. Upon winning the
$35,000*, a Gold Certificate will be
issued to the rider and a plaque with
his name and his horse's name will be
placed on the walls of the National
Cutting Horse Association's office.
These Non-Professionals have also
received Silver and Bronze Awards.

*1981—Amended to $100,000
*1985—Amended to $150,000

Richard Andersen, Salinas, California
Charlie Ashcraft, Decatur, Texas
Billy Baker, Hernando, Mississippi
Norman Bruce, Grayson, Georgia
M.L. Chartier, Fairhaven, Michigan
Randy Chartier, Fairhaven, Michigan
Carl M. Crawford, Indianola,
   Mississippi
Mitch Farris, Madisonville, Texas
Phil Feinberg, Paso Robles, California
David Gage, Wichita Falls, Texas
Dick Gaines, Byers, Texas
George W. Glover, Bay City, Texas
Tom Hastings, Denton, Texas
Lee Holsey, Corsicana, Texas
Mike Kelly, Electra, Texas
Wayland Long, Decatur, Texas
Jim Milner, Fort Worth, Texas
Mary Jo Milner, Irving, Texas
Tommy Moore, Mansfield, Texas
Debbie Patterson, Tecumseh,
   Oklahoma
John H. Paxton, Tallulah, Louisiana

Gil Porter, Lewisville, Texas
Mary Jo Reno, Simonton, Texas
Carol Rose, Gainesville, Texas
Larry Shearin, Creve Coeur, Missouri
Margie Suiter, Peoria, Arizona
Mrs. Buster Welch, Merkel, Texas

NCHA AFFILIATES

Acadian CHA
37039 White Rd.
Prairieville, LA 70769

Alamo Qtr Horse Breeders
739 Milam Bldg.
San Antonio, TX 78205

American Paint Horse Assn
P.O. Box 961023
Fort Worth, TX 76161

Area 18 CHA
Rt. 1 Box 494-A
Williamson, GA 30292

Arizona CHA
8034 E. Dale Lane
Scottsdale, AZ 85262

Ark-La-Tex CHA Inc.
P.O. Box 1116
Crockett, TX 75835

Ark-Mo CHA
P.O. Box 1581
Sikeston, MO 63801

Assoc. Nat'l Cavalos Apartacad
Prs. Prudente, SP 19100
Brazil 16100

Atlantic Coast CHA
P.O. Box 5251
High Point, NC 27262

Big Country CHA
Rt 1
Novice, TX 79538

Bluebonnet CHA
624 Fm 2754
Bellville, TX 77418

Brazoria Co CHA
P.O. Box 232
Sweeny, TX 77480

Brazos Valley Cutters, Inc.
P.O. Box 5026
Bryan, TX 77805

California CHA
2930 Chino Hills Pkwy.
Chino Hills, CA 91709

Canadian CHA
14141 Fox Drive
Edmonton, Alberta
Canada T6H 4P3

Caprock CHA
Rt 3 Box 181A
Post, TX 79356

Cascade Cow Cutters
21016 Shell Valley Way
Edmonds, WA 98020

Central Florida CHA
Rt 1 Box 232B
Lake Panasoffke, FL 33538

Central Illinois CHA
Rt 7 Box 5
Effingham, IL 62401

Central Michigan CHA
2990 Chickory Lane
Milford, MI 48042

Central Oklahoma CHA
Rt 3 Box 196K
Tecumseh, OK 74873

Central Texas CHA
P.O. Box 28
Elgin, TX 78621

Cotton States CHA
P.O. Box 580
Marshall, TX 75671

Cow Cutters CHA
Rt 2 Box 13
Anadarko, OK 73005

CHA of Nebraska
Rt 2 Box 60
Inavale, NE 68952

Delta CHA
Rt 2 Box 70
Tillar, AR 71670

East Coast CHA
Rt 2 Box 329-A
Lovettsville, VA 22080

East Tennessee CHA
Rt 3 Box 804
Spring City, TN 37381

Eastern Kansas CHA
Rt 1 Box 237
Herington, KS 67449

Eastern New Mexico CHA
1303 Breckon
Hobbs, NM 88240

El Paso CHA
Rt 1 Box 621
Anthony, NM 88021

Florida CHA
P.O. Box 70
Sumterville, FL 33585

Geneva CHA
Rt 1 Box 190
Hartford, AL 36344

Georgia CHA
Rt 1 Box 494 A
Williamson, GA 30292

Gold Coast CHA
P.O. Box 70
Sumterville, FL 33585

Gold Country CHA
3190 Muir
Yuba City, CA 95791

Greater New Mexico CHA
672 N St Rt
Questa, NM 87556

Hang Loose Cuttin Horse Assn.
1813 S. 14th Pl.
Rogers, AR 72756

Heart of Dixie CHA
2648 Pine Acres
Pike Road, AL 36064

Hill Country CHA
684 Johnson Dr.
Kerrville, TX 78028

Houston CHA
7518 Burgoyne #346
Houston, TX 77063

Idaho CHA
5196 Cree Cir
Boise, ID 83709

Illinois CHA
Rt 1 Box 100
Walnut Hill, IL 62893

Indiana CHA
3365 CR 53
Butler, IN 46721

Iowa CHA
Rt 3 Box 263
Coydon, IA 50060

Kansas CHA
2607 Schulman
Garden City, KS 67846

Kentucky CHA
4402 Routt Road
Louisville, KY 40299

Las Vegas CHA
3629 W. Hacienda
Las Vegas, NV 89118

Lone Star CHA
P.O. Box 407
Kemp, TX 75143

Louisiana CHA
37039 White Rd.
Prairieville, LA 70769

Lower South Carolina CHA
P.O. Box 60661
N. Charleston, SC 29419

Mid State CHA
#38 Andrew
England, AR 72046

Mid-South CHA
7386 Bethel Rd.
Olive Branch, MS 38654

Mid-State Illinois CHA
Rt 1 Box 166
Congerville, IL 61729

Middle Tennessee CHA
Rt. 2 Box 204
Puryear, TN 38251

Midwest Cutters, Inc.
Rt. 1 Box 34
Princeton, MO 64673

Minnesota CHA
Rt 2 Box 144
Northfield , MN 55057

Mississippi CHA
499 Pear Orchard Rd. #14A
Ridgeland, MS 39157

Missouri CHA
5799 Broadmoor #112
Mission, KS 66202

Montana CHA
78750 Gallatin Rd.
Bozeman, MT 59715

Moscow CHA c/o Show Place Arena
7582 Southern Ave.
Germantown, TN 38138

NCHA of Australia
P.O. Box 792 Tamworth, NSW
Australia 2340

National CHA of Germany
8224 Chieming
Germany

Nevada Reined Cow CHA
4705 Eastlake Blvd.
Carson City, NV 89704

New Zealand CHA
P.O. Box 1383
Taupo, N.I. New Zealand

North Alabama CHA
1409B Kathy Lane #6
Decatur, AL 35601

North Coast CHA
10511 Bartholomew Rd.
Chagrin Falls, OH 44022

North Dakota CHA
1100 Ward Rd.
Bismarck, ND 58501

North Mississippi CHA
P.O. Box 167
Batesville, MS 38606

North Texas CHA
Rt. 3 2300 Crusher Rd.
Jacksboro, TX 76056

Northeast Louisiana CHA
37039 White Rd.
Prairieville, LA 70769

Northeast Oklahoma CHA
Rt 2 Box 230
Chouteau, OK 74337

Northern Illinois CHA
19N975 Big Timber Rd.
Hampshire, IL 60140

Northern Piedmont CHA
9005 Sauls Rd.
Raleigh, NC 27603

Northwest CHA
P.O. Box 755
Camas, WA 98607

Nueces Canyon CHA
Rt 6 Box 6405
Brenham, TX 77833

Ohio CHA
2432 St. Rt. 753
Washington CH, OH 43160

Oil Belt CHA
119 Tiffany
Longview, TX 75601

Oklahoma CHA
615 Turner Lane #E8
Nowata, OK 74048

Oregon CHA
P.O. Box 755
Camas, WA 98607

Pacific Coast CHA
P.O. Box 15499
Sacramento, CA 95851

Panhandle CHA
HCR 1 Box 89
Wildorado, TX 79098

Pecos River CHA
P.O. Box 950
Gardendale, TX 79758

Pennsylvania CHA
Rt 4 Box 4651C
Spring Grove, PA 17362

Redwood Empire CHA
22900 River Rd.
Geyserville, CA 95441

Rose Country CHA
Rt 5 Box 278
Canton, TX 75103

San Diego County CHA
533 Amegos Rd.
Ramona, CA 92065

South Dakota CHA
Rt 1 Box 77A
Draper, SD 57531

Southeastern Oklahoma CHA
Rt. 2 Box 329A
McAlester, OK 74501

Southern Arizona CHA
3333 N. Silver Bell Rd.
Tucson, AZ 85745

Southern Cutters Assn.
P.O. Box 952
Unadilla, GA 31091

Southwestern Missouri CHA
Rt 1 Box 1657
Sarcoxie, MO 44862

Sowega CHA
2162 Hwy 280 W
Cordele, GA 31015

State of Missouri CHA
4000 Barberry
Columbia, MO 65202

Texas Gold Cutting -Athens
Rt 1 Box 918
Fairfield, TX 75840

Texas Gold Cutting-Waco
Rt. 1 Box 918
Fairfield, TX 75840

Tri-State CHA
Rt. 1
Green Castle, MO 63544

Utah CHA
2091 Somerset Dr.
Salt Lake City, UT 84121

Valley CHA
11435 Skyland Rd.
Sunland, CA 91040

Virginia CHA
Rt. 1 Box 18
Purcellville, VA 22132

Wateree CHA
Rt. 2 Box 263A
Johnston, SC 29832

West Central Texas, CHA
501 Rodeo Rd.
Graham, TX 76046

West Kentucky-Tennessee CHA
3010 Gracey-Herndon Rd.
Gracy, KY 42232

West Virginia CHA
Rt. 2 Box 237 A
Grafton, WV 26354

Western Oklahoma CHA
Rt. 2 Box 94
Roff, OK 74865

Western States CHA
29530 County Rd. Y
La Junta, CO 81050

Wyoming CHA
442 Lee Esther Ln.
Gillette, WY 82716

7-F CHA
Rt 1 Box 9
Midway, TX 75852

EXCUSES

Trainer

"My horse hates to use this ground."

"I judged him last week."

"After this, tell Zack to keep that dog out of the arena!"

"There's one judge who never read the rule book!"

"My wife forgot to enter me!"

"Need to start ridin' em more—*myself*!"

"She never really got used to a square pen."

"Got to quit workin' those sour cattle."

"It must be this bit!"

"Well—they all have their good days, and their bad days."

"We've been driving all night."

"No more grain—that's it—no more grain!"

"I think she needs more vitamins."

Non-Pro

"That judge *never* did like me."

"Well, I was doing great till I lost a cow."

"Geez—us ... Don't *ever* tell me to take a *Brahma* when I'm closing in on a *hereford*."

"He's never done that before!"

"Everyone's giving me the wrong advice!"

"Well, hell, I loped him for five hours!"

"I read an article on horses' vision the other day ...."

"68!! Shit, I've marked 75's on the same run!"

"Give me your honest opinion."

Amateur

"Give us a year."

"Told ya I needed a new saddle!"

"I tried a new experiment."

"My trainer says I need a new hat."

"I don't know ... But I *quit*! See ya all next week!"

"He's not used to this heat!"

"He's too fresh when it's cool."

"I thought it was a good run."

"I thought that's what Shorty meant!"

"We've been learning together."

Ladies

"She doesn't feel well today."

"She never has been broke to spurs."

"I think I need a new pair of chaps!"

"Is this judge partial to red shirts?"

Everyone

"Wait till I get home."

"She's never seen *Brahma* cattle before!"

"What do you mean, Hot Quit?"

"Next time don't talk to me when I'm in the herd!"

"Had 'em turned out all winter."

"Is she limping?"

"Hey! Does she look alright to you?"

"Those cattle last weekend really screwed him up!"

"I think their clock is wrong."

"I thought I was in the next bunch of cattle!"

"Worst cattle I ever cut!"

"Well, what do you think?"

"This always happens to me in this arena!"

"When did they come up with that rule?"

"Do you know anyone who wants to buy a good horse ... *cheap?*"

"That's it, that's it, scratch me from here on!"

"It's not her blind side, it's a blind judge!"

"I drew first again!"

"It's just *not* my day!"

Silent gestures

Rolling the eyes.

Kicking the ground.

Smashing your hat.

Training your horse immediately after the work.

Leaving the show a day early.

Going to the bathroom in your pants.

Taking the first offer.

PHOTO INDEX

Page 9
Julie Richmond.

9
Marvin Thomas saddling up in
Oakley, Utah.

10, 11
Cutting has its roots in ranch work
and at the small weekend cuttings
those roots feel close indeed. Here it
is, 30 miles of bad road to the nearest
town, Evanston, Wyoming. Here
Marvin Thomas is cutting at Deseret
Land and Livestock.

12, 13
Cutting practice at the Cottonwood
Canyon Ranch. By mid-summer in
the mountain states, most of the
cattle are on grass. Terry Hoffman has
traveled five hours from his office to
find fresh cattle.

14
Phil Green. The J. V. Ferry Feedlot,
Corinne, Utah, provides cutting in
deep sand.

15
Don Clark.

16
Lindsey Motley.

17
The Pacific Coast Cutting Horse
Association Challenge in Reno.

18
The Capitol Area Quarter Horse
Association Show at the Texas
Exposition and Heritage Center near
Austin. Outside, halter horses are
polished and admired, but it's inside
where the West begins.

19
Ray Lamb. St. George, Utah.

20
Paul Dunn. Rigby, Idaho.

21
Bob Mendenhall.

22
Jack McComber. PCCHA Challenge,
Reno, Nevada.

22
Bob Robinson. Cal-Ute Feedlot,
Delta, Utah.

23
Bob Condie. Deseret land and livestock.

23
When it's over, the horses go home,
and the cattle go back to their feeding
at the Harris Ranch, Coalinga,
California.

24
Bob Mendenhall at the Deseret Land
and Livestock Company.

41
Cutting horse sires often live in
exalted circumstances—temperature
controlled barns and white paddocks.
But not always. This is the stallion
station at the Fort Ranch. The horse,

Doc Rondo, has a desert view looking
toward the north shore of the Great
Salt Lake.

42
Broodmares and foals relax in a
pasture at Terry Riddle, Inc. in
Wynnewood, Oklahoma.

43
This foal is bred for athletic ability,
intelligence, and cow sense. The
desire to hunt a cow is in her blood.

44, 45
Horses bred for cutting are raised
almost free on Met and Lana
Johnson's Cottonwood Canyon
Ranch in southern Utah. Lana drove
the jeep, and it took a fast ride
through the sagebrush and up a rocky
creek bed to get within sight of this
herd of horses. The pastures are so
large the horses think they are wild.

46
The Fort Ranch Production Sale.
The bones of a deer attest to the
tough life in the rocky hills.

47
The sale is in late June, and the
babies are auctioned to the public.
Buyers return in the fall to pick up the
newly weaned, halter broke young
horses. The summer in the Fort
Ranch hills builds sure-footedness.

48
The NCHA Futurity Sale in Fort
Worth is at the Will Rogers Coliseum.
2 year old horses are worked on cattle
before cutting's most sophisticated
audience. Then they are sold at

auction. Greg Welch is the rider.

49
There are various cutting horse sales
during the NCHA Futurity in Fort
Worth. This is the Open Select Sale
at the John Justin Sales Arena.

50
Doug Jordan training a young futurity
prospect in a giant round pen at the
Stinchcomb Cattle Company in
Oklahoma.

51
This ranch cutting was in Antimony,
Utah. Because the closest motel is 40
miles away down a dirt road, many
cutters spend the night in tents or
campers. As they saddle and warm
up their horses in the early morning,
the ranch cowboys bring in the cattle
that soon will be used in the contest,
and many cutters go out to join in the
cattle penning.

52
Sue Lind is in the herd.

53
Marvin Thomas cutting at the Lind
Ranch, Marion, Utah. Summer is
short and very special in the High
Valleys at the Rockies western edge.

54
Venture Farms/Caribou Creek Ranch,
Ellensberg, Washington.

55
Bill Freeman working a futurity
prospect at his ranch near Rosston,
Texas. The fences and walls, the
rodeo chutes, and the arena size all

duplicate the arena in the Will Rogers Coliseum, where the NCHA Futurity is held. Bill leaves no doubt about the focus of his program.

56
Mike Mascaro.

57
Jerry Quillian.

58
Gene Hintze.

59
The Pacific Coast Cutting Horse Association Futurity at the Los Angeles Equestrian Center in Griffith Park, in Burbank, California is surrounded by freeways and city. Gary Ray is tuning a horse in the practice arena.

60
Bob Robinson at Deseret Land and Livestock.

60
Bob Robinson, St. George, Utah.

61
Fred Hunter in Mesquite, Nevada on a cold day in February. Cow, horse, and man all are in their winter coats.

62
In the herd, the movements are slow and careful. Looks are exchanged between selector and selectee.

63
Canyon Country, California. Hollywood stuntman, Billy Burton, showing a horse.

64
Tremonton, Utah.

65
The typical cutting saddle has a flat seat, full double rigging and oxbow stirrups.

66
The Harris Ranch in central California is a cutter's paradise, a feedlot with thousands of fresh cows. During the cutting, the air strip next to the restaurant is full of private jets. In the early morning, the valley floor is filled with bugs. Many riders and a few horses had bandanas over their noses and mouths to keep the insects out. But, as the day warmed up, the bandanas disappeared.

67
Chubby Turner loosens a cinch.

67
Cutters and kabitzers wait their turn.

68
Lind Ranch cutting, Marion, Utah.

69
Oakley Rodeo grounds under the watchful eye of the Mormon Church.

70
Austin, Texas...you can study cows a lifetime and still not be sure what they will do.

71, 72
Cattle.

81
Jim Reno, sculptor, western artist, and

past president of the NCHA, working a young horse in the cool early morning near Kerrville, Texas.

82
The arena at the Oak Crest Ranch near Fort Worth is like a giant covered sandbox. There will be action here soon.

83
Cheryl Dennie Bryant tuning at the Oak Crest Ranch. One horse was a little fresh and threatened to buck when she started cutting. Cheryl just laughed.

84
Buster Welch at dawn. The best cutting horses are trained with a lot of patience. There's plenty of time to wait ... and think.

85
Buster Welch cutting.

86
The cook house/guest house porch at Buster Welch's ranch near Merkel, Texas. The porch is part old saddle and photo museum, part shade for watching arena action. There is a lot of cutting history here.

87
Buster Welch, practice at sunup.

88
Leonard Davis puts on a side pull training device at the McDaniel Ranch, Phoenix, Arizona.

89
Doug Jordan training a young futurity

horse in Oklahoma.

90
Jim Emerson, Gainesville, Texas.

91
Colin Miller at the Malad, Idaho rodeo grounds.

92
Francisco Zamora, Salina, Utah.

93
Springtime has finally come to snow country—cutting at Terry Hymas' place in Ovid, Idaho. Steve Olsen showing.

94
Jeannie Fullen selects a cow in Malad, Idaho. Very careful slow work here can set things up just right. A misstep or wrong choice can lead to a full speed wreck.

95
Colin Miller at the J.V. Ferry Feedlot.

96
Kevin Dwyer. Peppermill Cutting, Mesquite, Nevada.

97
Left to right, top to bottom: Buster Welch in his training pen; Doug Jordan; Focused rider tuning at the Tropicana Hotel; Bob Robinson judging at Spanish Fork, Utah; Paula Gaughan; Shane Prescott; Ascencion Banuelos and Frank Frazier, Jr. in Burbank at the tuning pens; Russell McCord and other cutters watching the competition at the NCHA Futurity; and Debbie McGregor,

judge, making the draw.

98, 99
Neil Webb.

100
The practice pens, PCCHA Futurity in Burbank, California. Jan Outman working.

101
Action in the tuning pens in Reno, Nevada. This is cow country's traditional sport in a high-tech environment. In this room of cement and pipe, the imported dirt seems strangely out of place.

102
Mike Lowery in the tuning pens at the Tropicana Hotel. There were three tuning pens—red, yellow, and green—and they were in constant action, dawn to dusk. The actual cutting took place inside the hotel on the tennis courts.

103
Luke Bakey tuning in Burbank.

104, 105
Rain and misery won't drive the cutters home, but danger to the horses' legs might. A sandy arena may retain good footing even when quite wet, but a clay arena can get slick, puddle, and flood ... and end a cutting. Brent Layton, Paul Mendenhall, Bob Condie, and Bob Mendenhall in their matching yellow outfits.

106
This horse trailer tack closet reveals

that trophy saddles get used.

106
Bill Freeman's tack room reveals a lot too, including rope.

107
The well dressed cutter wears a trophy buckle and spurs. They come in a variety of styles and shapes.

108
Lindy Burch turning back for Chubby Turner, who is cutting at the Harris Ranch. Lindy's job is to keep the cow's attention on the cutter, until he wants off.

109
Rick Mowery cutting at the Harris Ranch. Tim Stewart is the corner man or herd holder. His job is to keep the herd centered on the back fence and to help position the cattle during the initial cut. He sometimes can prevent disaster on the wall.

110
The novice classes usually are later in the day. Amy Lind showing.

111
St. George, Utah.

112
Fred Hunter.

121
Cow cutting's biggest event is Finals night of the NCHA Futurity in Fort Worth's Will Rogers Coliseum, which is awash with cutting horse history. Here, the best bred, best trained horses are ridden by legendary riders,

competing with the best cattle for big money.

122
At the NCHA Super Stakes Classic, cutters wait for the cattle change to go in or out.

122
Bill Glass, Tom Lyons, Lindy Burch, and Bill Freeman watch the cattle, looking for cows they might like ... and for ones they might like to avoid.

122
The herd is settled for 20 minutes before the action starts, so the cattle will be calm and comfortable at the end of the arena.

123
Larry Reeder at the Will Rogers Coliseum, Fort Worth.

124, 125
Transportation can get fancy for both horse and man. There is a lot of money in the parking lot at a cutting, especially Fort Worth.

126
Freddie McGee.

126
Roy Carter, at the Super Stakes Classic.

127
Greg Welch.

128
Rick Mowery at the NCHA Futurity.

129
The Futurity audience is

knowledgeable, enthusiastic and noisy. The tension and spirit is like that at a title fight, or the Super Bowl. There are furs, diamonds and cowboy hats in this crowd.

130, 131
The view from the catwalk above the lights at the Will Rogers Coliseum: the cutting becomes a ballet from here, horses and cows in an abstract dance. It's a very hot, very dusty, cramped place from which to watch ... and it's a long way down.

132
Ronnie Rice, NCHA Futurity Open Finals, Fort Worth.

133
Herd work. Greg Welch.

134
Bill Freeman, Open Semifinals, the NCHA Futurity.

135
Frank Craighead.

136
Cutters waiting to leave.

136
The Will Rogers Equestrian Center is a giant horse complex. Besides the huge arena, seats and parking lots there are underground passages, sale rings, tuning pens, stalls and this horse shower where several horses can bathe at once.